For Sophomores in Reading 2

Power Skills in Writing — I

Power Skills in Writing — I

Roger B. Goodman
William Ince

A Trafalgar House Book
McGraw-Hill Book Company
New York, St. Louis, San Francisco, Auckland, Bogotá, Düsseldorf, Johannesburg, London, Madrid, Mexico, Montreal, New Delhi, Panama, Paris, São Paulo, Singapore, Sydney, Tokyo, and Toronto

Copyright ©1979, Trafalgar House Publishing, Inc.

Printed in the United States of America

All rights reserved. No part of this book may be reproduced or transmitted in any form or by any means, electronic or mechanical, including photocopying, recording, or any information storage and retrieval system, without permission in writing from the Publisher.

Trafalgar House Publishing, Inc.
145 East 52nd Street, New York, New York 10022

Library of Congress Cataloging in Publication Data

Printing: 1 2 3 4 5 6 7 8 9   Year: 9 0 1 2 3 4 5 6 7 8

ERRATA SHEET—POWER SKILLS IN WRITING—I

Page 5. Q.47
47. (1) villain   (3) statute
    (2) siege   (4) occurs

Page 8. 1st Line
x   tax, mix, ox—ks   Xerox, xylophone—z

Page 24. Exercise One, Q.1
1. "When Irish eyes are smilin'..." is a line from a popular
         $\underline{1}$ $\underline{2}$ $\underline{3}$
   $\underline{song}$.
   $\overline{4}$

Page 25. Exercise One, Q.4
4. The mayor of beirut rules a ruined city.
   $\overline{1}$ $\overline{2}$ $\overline{3}$ $\overline{4}$

Page 25. Exercise One, Q.5
5. Her favorite drink is Coca-cola.
   $\overline{1}$ $\overline{2}$ $\overline{3}$ $\overline{4}$

Page 27. Exercise Four, Q.1
1. at one time, the Chrysler Building was the tallest building
   $\overline{1}$ $\overline{2}$ $\overline{3}$ $\overline{4}$
   in the world.

Page 29. Rule Fifteen
RULE FIFTEEN: All abbreviations for names and titles are capitalized:

Page 29. Exercise Six, Q.2
2. The latter was away for a holiday at camp David.
   $\overline{1}$ $\overline{2}$ $\overline{3}$ $\overline{4}$

Page 30. Exercise Six, Q.10
10. He wrote a letter saying:

    Dear Dad,
    $\overline{1}$

    I'm planning to become a hamburger.
                              $\overline{2}$

    Your son,
    $\overline{3}$ $\overline{4}$

    Harvard

Page 31. Q.8
8. Great We've won the final game of the series

Page 35. Rule Three
Observe the preceding sentence carefully. Reread it, this time omitting all absolutely non-essential material. What should result is:

Page 36. Exercise Three, Q. 9

9. Witnesses What do they know

Page 39. Q. 8

8. Then one goes to Shakespeare Physician heal thyself

Page 54. Q. 9

9. The women jockeys won (?) places on the circuit.

Page 78. Q. 6

6. But since he was annoyed, all I said only served to (aggravate, irritate) the situation.

Page 98. Q. 24

24. *Feeling it was shameful, their language was criticized by all.*

(1) Their language, feeling it was shameful, was criticized.
(2) Their language was criticized shamefully by all.
(3) Their language, feeling it was shameful, they all criticized it.
(4) Feeling their language was shameful, they all criticized it.
(5) no change

Page 111. Para. 2

tune or a familiar dance beat. If the band threw a waltz beat into a cha-cha, everyone would respond immediately, probably by stumbling all over the place!

Page 113. Complex Sentences

ival or *adverbial* in function. One way to spot the dependent clauses will be to notice the relative pronouns—*who, whom, what, that, which*—for adjectival clauses and the subordinating conjunctions—*when, if, since, because, where*—and others for the adverbial clauses. Watch:

Page 117. Q. 10

10. Taking drugs, clearly, does not solve problems.

Page 119. Q. 2

2. There was *hardly nothing* he didn't know about the use of the tools.

Page 120. Q. 8

8. After the fourth inning, the coach read the team the riot act, bawled out the pitcher, and *encouraged* the team to do its best.

(1) urged
(2) exhorted
(3) coerced
(4) wanted
(5) no change

Page 121. Q. 12
(1) "What's the row all about?"
(2) "I guess I'm in trouble, anyway."
(3) "I could care less!"
(4) "So what?"
(5) no change

Page 127. Line 8
This rule is honored more in the books than in everyday language. Just as "It's me." has come to be accepted in common language, so has the occasional split infinitive.

Page 130. Q. 6
6. In sentence 2, the word *woman* should be

Page 131. Q. 10
10. Sentence 2 should
(1) be connected to Sentence 1 as it stands
(2) be made into two sentences
(3) begin the paragraph
(4) be connected to Sentence 3 by the word *also*
(5) no change, except as in question 9 above

Page 148. *tude* Suffix

| tude | quality of | noun | magnitude |

Page 151. Q. 2
3. (1) intelligent (3) advise
   (2) supervice   (4) won't

Page 153. Q. 4
4. Maria and Kathy waited breathlessly for the announce-
   $\overline{}$ $\overline{}$
   1   2
   ment, both girls hoping she had won the high award.
                    $\overline{}$ $\overline{}$
                    3   4

Page 156. Q. 2
2. The policeman said the suspect had *transgressed* the law as he saw it.

Page 158. Q. 12
12. "This little fellow," he said, "is cute, smart, and *perspicacious*."

Page 168. Exercise Four, A.5,6
5. titles'
6. wolves'

Page 169. Exercise One, A.5
5. (4) The entire name of the product is Coca-Cola.

Page 170. Exercise Six, A. 4
4. (5) Correct as is.

Page 172. Exercise Three, A. 10
10. When one fully considers all the facts, November 14, 1492, will be one of history's great dates.

Page 172. Exercise Four, A. 5
5. Love can lead us to say strange things; love can make us do stranger things.

Page 174. Exercise Five, A. 2
2. *Who* did you say taught you how to throw a pass? (You said he taught you —thus, *who*.)

Page 177. Exercise Seventeen, A. 6
6. But since he was annoyed, all I said only served to *aggravate* the situation.

Page 179. Pretest, A. 2
2. (5) The sentence is correct as is.

Page 179. Pretest, A. 22
22. (4) Two elements are involved here keeping the tenses consistent in the past and eliminating the dangling participle.

Page 182. Pretest, A. 2
2. (1) This removes the double negative.

Page 183. A. 8
8. (2) *Exhorted* expresses the emotion that is described.

Page 183. A. 18
18. (2) It is again a matter of tone.

Page 184. Pretest, A. 6
6. (1) It is clear that the plural sense is required.

Page 184. Pretest, A. 10
10. (5) Change suggested in #9 above.

Page 188. Posttest, A. 2
2. (5)

Page 189. Diction and Style, A. 1
1. (3) Since we are speaking about a "gang," the level of speech is probably lower than that indicated by the other choices. This is slang.

Page 189. Diction and Style, A. 2
2. (3) The other choices are too formal.

Page 190. A. 12
12. (3) It is clear that this conclusion culminates the thought of the paragraph.

Contents

Introduction vii
1. Spelling 1
2. Capitalization 23
3. Punctuation 31
4. Grammar and Usage 41
5. Sentence Structure 93
6. Diction and Style 119
7. Logic and Organization 129
8. Vocabulary 145
9. Posttest 151
10. Answers and Analysis 165

Introduction

This book is part of a series which has been written to help you receive practice in understanding questions which you may find on many of the tests you will take throughout your school years. Regardless of the nature of the examination, it is likely that the types of questions you will find in this book will appear in some form on that test.

    If you study and use this book in the way it was prepared to be used, either by yourself or in a study group, or under a teacher's direction, you will find that you will soon be able to answer most of the questions correctly. When you check your answers, go over the explanations to the correct answers. You will notice a pattern in the types of questions that are asked. When you complete all of the passages in one section, go on to the next group.

TEST-TAKING TECHNIQUES

It is almost as important for the student to know *how to take a test* as it is to know the content or subject matter that is being tested. There are some very basic procedures that students need to know about taking tests, whether they are taking the high school equivalency examination, a college entrance test, a civil service exam, or an achievement, placement, or aptitude test.

GENERAL RECOMMENDATIONS FOR TEST-TAKING

1. *Survey the test* by taking a quick look at the entire test to get an idea of the kinds of questions that are asked, the general content, and the levels of difficulty. On some standardized tests, the questions get more difficult at the end of a given passage. Read each question carefully and base your answers on the information that is either stated in the passage or inferred from the passage, according to the choices given.

2. *Be aware of time.* Work carefully and quickly and be aware of the time that is given for a particular section and for the entire test. Watch for indications of time signals. Check to see if the passage of time is listed on the board and how much time you will have for the remainder of the test or the section of the test that you are working on. Be prepared by bringing your own stopwatch or wristwatch.

3. *Check for specifics.* Scan the content and try to notice whether a question refers to a particular line, sentence, or quotation. Watch for *test traps* and be careful to read and follow test instructions. Be certain that you follow specific directions for each section.

4. *Read the questions first.* Glance at the questions that accompany the passage before you read the selection. If you do so, your mind will store the questions for you, and as you read the passage your brain will recall or retrieve the answers to the questions that your memory has stored.

Remember that in any reading test, your purpose for reading is to answer questions based on specific selections.

5. *Select appropriate answers.* Watch out for answers that seem too easy, and make sure that you notice similarities in answer choices. Again, check for tricks. *When more than one answer seems correct*, reread the

information in the passage to determine the correct, most accurate, most complete, or most appropriate answer.

6. *Make the most of your time.* Although intelligent, well-thought out responses are best, *you should know when to guess.* If you are having difficulty in answering a particular question based on a given selection, don't waste time. Go on to the other questions and, if time permits, return to the question that is giving you difficulty. If the difficulty in making a choice continues, relax and make an "educated" guess." Remember *not* to leave any questions unanswered.

Finally, remember that this is a test of your ability to read, to follow directions, and to use all of the skills and test-taking techniques that you have learned. Have confidence in your ability to pass.

Now that you have been introduced to this book, take the pretest, score it, and begin working on the content sections. Good luck!

Power Skills in Writing — I

ONE

Spelling

PRETEST

In each of the following groups of words, one may be misspelled. In the answer column, blacken the space that is the same as the number of the misspelled word. If no word is misspelled, blacken space 5.

1. (1) attendence (3) murdered
   (2) juvenile   (4) obstacle

2. (1) politician (3) absolutly
   (2) similar   (4) glossary

3. (1) emigrant   (3) unduly
   (2) reciever   (4) egotism

4. (1) commercial (3) diamond
   (2) mattress   (4) liesure

5. (1) survival   (3) species
   (2) labratory   (4) women

6. (1) lightening (3) fourth
   (2) forty   (4) ninety

7. (1) contagious (3) scarsely
   (2) man's   (4) digital

WRITING

8. (1) decision
   (2) ommit
   (3) forth
   (4) committed

9. (1) signifigant
   (2) adversely
   (3) universal
   (4) won't

10. (1) concrete
    (2) generous
    (3) gorgeous
    (4) immense

11. (1) appearence
    (2) villain
    (3) finally
    (4) witness

12. (1) peaceful
    (2) peice
    (3) parent
    (4) fifth

13. (1) morale
    (2) miracle
    (3) curiousity
    (4) moral

14. (1) discipline
    (2) concept
    (3) decieve
    (4) divided

15. (1) census
    (2) their
    (3) they're
    (4) there

16. (1) metropolitan
    (2) environment
    (3) meerly
    (4) merciful

17. (1) beautiful
    (2) prey
    (3) happyness
    (4) therefore

18. (1) opponent
    (2) truly
    (3) arguement
    (4) courteous

19. (1) papal
    (2) fatel
    (3) alter
    (4) neither

20. (1) similiar
    (2) familiar
    (3) wield
    (4) ninth

SPELLING

21. (1) all right (3) allthough
    (2) always (4) thorough

22. (1) breakfast (3) arable
    (2) edible (4) sympethy

23. (1) benifit (3) whole
    (2) worthy (4) athlete

24. (1) attached (3) prefer
    (2) begining (4) always

25. (1) faculty (3) desease
    (2) facility (4) corps

26. (1) concede (3) fourty
    (2) fourth (4) appeal

27. (1) presede (3) interfere
    (2) preference (4) appall

28. (1) scenery (3) offen
    (2) wealth (4) either

29. (1) site (3) sight
    (2) sleigh (4) cite

30. (1) convienient (3) corpse
    (2) eminent (4) imminent

31. (1) interfere (3) illegal
    (2) reffered (4) although

32. (1) sophmore (3) calendar
    (2) February (4) escape

33. (1) enviorment (3) veil
    (2) pioneers (4) respectable

WRITING

34.
(1) physical
(2) philosophy
(3) medecal
(4) Wednesday

35.
(1) rhyme
(2) affect
(3) effective
(4) rythm

36.
(1) assistance
(2) personnel
(3) offerring
(4) doesn't

37.
(1) goes
(2) imposing
(3) exciteing
(4) exit

38.
(1) fifth
(2) isn't
(3) it's
(4) impossable

39.
(1) hopeful
(2) roping
(3) trapping
(4) writting

40.
(1) noticable
(2) believe
(3) noticing
(4) cringing

41.
(1) foundry
(2) boundries
(3) author
(4) dinner

42.
(1) almost
(2) absense
(3) truthful
(4) happily

43.
(1) heroes
(2) flying
(3) trys
(4) Almighty

44.
(1) describe
(2) referred
(3) preference
(4) nicly

45.
(1) disease
(2) underneath
(3) deceit
(4) certian

46.
(1) desperate
(2) truly
(3) seperate
(4) difference

SPELLING

47. (1) villain   (3) statute
    (2) seige   (4) occurrs

48. (1) privilege   (3) sincerely
    (2) proffessor (4) stopping

49. (1) height   (3) neice
    (2) explanation (4) leisure

50. (1) rediculous (3) writing
    (2) eighty   (4) practice

51. (1) surprise   (3) suddeness
    (2) surely   (4) vegetable

52. (1) tragedy   (3) pastime
    (2) studied   (4) equiptment

53. (1) success   (3) posess
    (2) pleasant   (4) prejudice

54. (1) seize   (3) corporal
    (2) sergeant   (4) requirment

55. (1) safty   (3) optimist
    (2) scarcely   (4) woman

56. (1) personal   (3) noticeable
    (2) mathematics (4) managment

57. (1) potatoes   (3) eligible
    (2) embarrassing (4) hoping

58. (1) trespassing (3) alleys
    (2) accidentally (4) amatuer

59. (1) almost   (3) descent
    (2) couragous   (4) decent

60. (1) conscience   (3) dialogue   60. 1 2 3 4 5
    (2) definately   (4) believable

SPELLING RULES

Rules were not made to be broken; they were made to help. Sometimes you can make up your own spelling rules or tricks that will help you to remember how to spell. The real test of a rule is very simple—if it works, it is right.

A Simple Sequence for Spelling

1. SEE the word—remember what it *looks* like.
2. SAY the word—watch for tricky pronunciation.
3. WRITE the word—remember what it *looks* like.

Sound Clues

In terms of sound, English is a puzzling language. Not all words sound the way they look. There are letter combinations that can fool you. But, once again, there are rules of pronunciation that can help in most cases. What follows is a listing of all the letters of the alphabet. For each letter you will find two keys: *primary*, the sound more often used; and *secondary*, the sound less often found.

Letter	Primary	Secondary
a	1. at, cap, hat—short *a* 2. ate, cape, hate—the long or *name* sound	affect, abuse—*uh*
b	but, absent, crab—a gentle, punched lip sound that changes	
c	1. cell, decent, city— *s* (To be sounded like an *s*, letter *c* must be followed by *e*, *i*, or *y*.) 2. can, helicopter, cut—*k* (To be sounded like a *k*, the letter *c* must be followed by *a*, *o*, *t*, or *u*.	1. cello—*ch* 2. vicious—*sh*
d	dog, bad, addition—the *d* is a hard, unchanging sound formed by the tongue and the upper gum	

SPELLING

e	1. red, men—short *e* (*eh*) 2. be, even—the long or *name* sound
f	final, for, off—a sharp, pushed sound made with breath, lips, and teeth of—a *v* sound made by lips and teeth
g	1. go, bag, grab—hard *g* (must be followed by a consonant, or *a, i, o,* or *u*) 2. age gorgeous, prestige—soft *g*—or *gj* (must be followed by *e*, or sometimes *i*)
h	hotel, hope, hurricane—a heavy blowing out between parted lips. The sound of the letter *h* is like an outward breath.
i	1. fin, sin, kin—short *i* (*ih*) 2. fine, sine, kite—long or *name* sound
j	jog, ajar—a hard, pushed sound (*dj*) made by teeth, tongue, and voice
k	kick, joke—a clicking sound at the back of the throat; a hard *c*
l	lull, lollipop—a soft lulling sound made by tongue behind upper teeth, plus voice
m	mama, amuse—a humming sound made by placing lips together and using voice
n	never, seen—made by parting lips, teeth apart, tongue behind upper teeth, and voice
o	1. mop, top, cop—short *o* 2. mope, cope—long or name sound
p	pupil, pope—formed by popping breath through lips
q	queen, aqua—(note: In spelling, *q* is always followed by *u*.) Pronounced like *k* with a *w* sound following: *kw*.
r	roar, arrest—a growling sound in the back of the throat
s	1. same, stamp, thrust—sharp *s*; hiss 2. **mission, fission, tissue**— *sh*
t	hit, tub, battle—tongue behind upper gum, lips and teeth parted, sharp outward breath 1. nation, fracture—*sh* 2. capture—*ch*
u	1. cut, run, dun—short *u* (*uh*) 2. cute, dune—long or name sound
v	violin, van, violence—teeth on lips, voiced sound
w	wind, away—shaping sound with little voice or breath

x	tax, mix, ox—*ks*	
y	you, yawn—a pushed-through sound	1. silly, cith—*ee* 2. myth—short *i* (*ih*) 3. rhyme—long *i*
z	zone, zero—heavy, long *s*	

Vowels and Consonants

Among the terms frequently used when we discuss spelling are VOWEL and CONSONANT. There are only six vowels: *a*, *e*, *i*, *o*, *u*, and sometimes *y* (myth, mystery, rhythm). All the other letters in the alphabet are consonants.

There are certain combinations of letters that should be fixed in your mind. They assist in both pronunciation and spelling: phth—di*phth*eria (pronounced dif-theria); *ph*iloso*phy* (ph—f); *psy*chology (psy—si).

Now let us go to some of the actual rules. Remember that even though the rules do not work all the time, they are very reliable guides.

RULE ONE: (This is probably the best known and the most easily remembered.)

I before E
Except after C
Or when sounded like "ay"
As in n*ei*ghbor or w*ei*gh.

There are several important words in which this rule does not work: seize, either, neither, weird, leisure, financier, foreign, and height.

EXERCISE ONE

In each of the following groups of words, one may be misspelled. In the answer column, blacken the space that has the same number as the misspelled word. If no word is misspelled, blacken space 5.

Sample: 1. perceive   **2. deciet**   3. chief   4. belief

1. (1) recieve   (3) brief   1. 1 2 3 4 5
   (2) conceive   (4) belief

2. (1) seize   (3) cheif   2. 1 2 3 4 5
   (2) grief   (4) friend

SPELLING

3. (1) height   (3) frieght
   (2) piece   (4) neither

4. (1) reign   (3) piece
   (2) neice   (4) cashier

5. (1) achieve   (3) pierce
   (2) mien   (4) seige

6. (1) feirce   (3) yield
   (2) foreign   (4) believer

7. (1) brief   (3) feind
   (2) sleigh   (4) veil

8. (1) conceit   (3) pier
   (2) neither   (4) retreive

9. (1) grief   (3) leisure
   (2) shriek   (4) weird

10. (1) heir   (3) mischeif
    (2) their   (4) priest

RULE TWO: In words ending with a *y* that comes just after a consonant, change the *y* to *i* before adding *es*, *ed*, *er*, and *est*.

    try: tri-es; tri-ed—tries, tried
    country: countri-es—countries
    boundary: boundari-es—boundaries
    happy: happi-er; happi-est—happier, happiest

RULE THREE: In words ending with a *y* that comes just after a consonant, change the *y* to *i* before adding *ly*, *ness*, *ful*.

    sloppy: sloppi-ly—sloppily
    happy: happi-ness—happiness
    fancy: fanci-ful—fanciful

RULE FOUR: In words ending with a *y* that comes just after a vowel, simply add *s* to *form the plural* or to show *the present tense.*

    say-s—says
    day-s—days
    monkey-s—monkeys
    Sunday-s—Sundays

EXERCISE TWO

Use the rules you have just learned in changing the following words:

1. He wore the (fancy-est) jeans I have ever seen.   1. _____
2. I wouldn't wear them even on (Sunday-s).   2. _____
3. He is a real (worry-er).   3. _____
4. The umpires set the (boundary-es) for the game.   4. _____
5. It's hard to say what (happy-ness) really is.   5. _____
6. Thirty (day-s) hath September.   6. _____
7. They put fences around both (quarry-es).   7. _____
8. It is great to have (Wednesday-s) off.   8. _____
9. It is even greater to have all (day-s) off.   9. _____
10. I must say that they (try-ed) as hard as they could.   10. _____

RULE FIVE: In words ending with a silent *e*, we keep the *e* when adding any syllable beginning with a consonant.

    encourage-ment—encouragement
    hope-ful—hopeful
    life-less—lifeless
    lone-ly—lonely
    nice-ly—nicely

SPELLING

RULE SIX: In words ending with a silent *e*, we drop the *e* before syllables beginning with vowels, unless we want to have a *soft g* (*dj*) or a *soft c* (*s*) sound.

    believe-able—believable
    hope-ing—hoping
    tape-ing—taping

but

    courage-ous—courageous
    manage-able—manageable
    notice-able—noticeable
    singe-ing—singeing (This means burning slightly.)

Note: The name *Gorgeous George* is a good illustration of the "G-rule."

Note: Occasionally, adding *ing* makes for an exception:

    cringe-ing—cringing
    discourage-ing—discouraging
    notice-ing—noticing

RULE SEVEN: In certain words, when we add *ed*, *er*, or *ing* and we want to keep the short vowel sound, we double the final consonant.

    hop-ing—hopping
    tap-ing—tapping (The word *taping* has a long *a* sound and means using tape; the word *tapping*—with a short *a*—refers to the sound.)

In each case, if we simply added the *ing*, we would retain the long (name) sound of the vowel, and the word would be entirely different.

EXERCISE THREE

In each of the following words, add the indicated syllable, applying the correct rule:

1. He gave her no (encourage-ing) signs.   1. _____

2. She was, however, forever (hope-ful).   2. _____

3. Chasing him gave her some of her (happy-est) moments.   3. _____

4. He always made (disparage-ing) remarks in her presence.   4. _____

5. These made her chase him even more (intense-ly).   5. _____

6. All her (hope-ing) kept him (hop-ing). 6. _____

7. His distance made him more (desire-able) than ever. 7. _____

8. Even his not (notice-ing) her caused no (cringe-ing) in her manner. 8. _____

9. She never thought of (replace-ing) him in her heart. 9. _____

10. She acted as though she had never heard a (discourage-ing) word. 10. _____

RULE EIGHT: Some words with two syllables end with a vowel just before the consonant. If the accent is on the *second syllable*, we *double the final consonant* when we add *er* or *ing*.

refer-ed—referred; but reference (It is reference because the accent shifts to the first syllable.)
prefer-ing—preferring; but preference
deter-ence—deterrence
infer-ing—inferring; but inference

RULE NINE: We sometimes find difficulty in forming the plurals of certain nouns. But the rules can and do help. Most plurals are made by adding *s* or *es* to the singular form:

dog-s—dogs
house-s—houses
box-es—boxes

Most words that end with *ch*, *s*, *sh*, *x*, and *z* form their plurals by adding *es*:

wish-es—wishes
church-es—churches
sex-es—sexes

Some plurals are formed by making changes *within* the word itself:

child—children
loaf—loaves
man—men
mouse—mice
tooth—teeth
wife—wives

wolf—wolves
woman—women (remember the plural for "man")

RULE TEN: And now for a positive negative! The apostrophe is *not* used to form the plural. The apostrophe is used to show possession:

boy—boy's hat
country—country's flag
women—women's purses

Note: If the word ends with an *s*, the apostrophe comes after the *s*:

boys—boys' hats (many boys; many hats)
bus—bus'

Note: Since the possessive form of words like *bus* is pronounced as though there were the additional *s*, it is sometimes actually added:

bus's license number

And now the exception: To form a very special kind of plural, the apostrophe is used. If we say the letter *s* appears four times in the word *possess*, we may write, "There are four *s*'s in the word *possess*." (Remember that for spelling!) The same is true for numbers: "Three *6*'s make eighteen."

EXERCISE FOUR

Form the plural possessive of the following words:

1. housewife
2. fieldmouse
3. bat
4. person
5. title
6. wolf
7. woman
8. lady

WRITING

9. our 9. _____

10. child 10. _____

EXERCISE FIVE

Add ed *or* ing *to the following words:*

1. suffer 1. _____

2. refer 2. _____

3. interfere 3. _____

4. inter 4. _____

5. prefer 5. _____

6. monitor 6. _____

7. audit 7. _____

8. differ 8. _____

9. defer 9. _____

10. offer 10. _____

RULE ELEVEN: To form the plural of words ending in *o* preceded by a vowel, add *s*:

    patio-s—patios
    radio-s—radios
    ratio-s—ratios
    studio-s—studios

RULE TWELVE: To form the plural of words ending in *o* after a consonant, there is something of a problem:

  1. Some words add *es*:   echo-es—echoes
                                          hero-es—heroes

SPELLING

2. Some words add *s*:
  potato-es—potatoes
  tomato-es—tomatoes
  dynamo-s—dynamos
  piano-s—pianos
  soprano-s—sopranos

3. Some words add either *s* or *es*:
  motto-s, es—mottos, mottoes
  tornado-s, es—tornados, tornadoes
  zero-s, es—zeros, zeroes

EXERCISE SIX

Change all of the underlined words to plural form. Watch for possessives.

The hero zero were all shot down during tornado. On the ground they went down like domino. All their theory of flight were upset by their leader remarks. They treated the principle of formation flying like old wife tales. But they all became ace.

SPELLING LISTS

Following are three lists of words, broken down in order of relative difficulty. The parts of the words indicated in LARGE LETTERS are there to provide eye and ear clues for spelling. Don't try to memorize great numbers of words at a time; keep the list handy for reference while you are studying.

Easier But Confusing Words

absence
absoLUTELY
acceptABLE
accidentALLY (accident-al-ly)
accompanying
account
accumUlate
accuRATELY

acCUSTOM
achiEVEment
across
address
adjournment
adVICE (noun)
adVISE (verb)
AGREEment

aisle
all right (*always* two words)
almost
appearANCE
arGUMent (NOTE: argue)
ARRANGEment
artICLE
aTHLete (aTHLetic)
attaCHed
attenDANCE
auDIBLE
auTHOR

basicALLY
begINNING
beLIEve (beLIEF)
BURYing

capTAIN
CAReer
CAREfully
cerTAIN
CHIEF
CHOSEn
COMing
conSCIENCE
conSCIENTIous
conSCIOUS
correspondENCE
courAGEous
COURTeous
CRITICism

DAIry (milk)
deCEIT
deCENT (good)
DEcision (DEcide)
defendANT

deFINITEly
deSCEND (to go down)
descendANT
DEscription (DEscribe)
desIRAble
DEspair
desPERate
dialoGUE
differENCE
DINing (dine-ing)
DINNer (what one eats)
DISeased (sick)
DOESn't

EIGHT
eligIBLE
embARRASS (and: embarrassing; embarrassment)
EMinent (noteworthy)
emphaSIZE
eQUIPment
eQUIPPED
exAGGErate
exCEED (proceed; succeed)
exCELLent
existENCE
exPLANation (but: exPLAIN)
EXTRAordinary
EXTREMEly

famiLIAR (from: family)
FebRUary
FIEry (FIErce)
finALLY
financIER
foREIGN
FORty (but: FOURth)
FOURteen
friEND

fulFILL

GOVERNment
gramMAR
GRUEsome
GUard
guiDANCE

HEIGHT
herOES
HOPing (from: hope)
HOPPing (from: hop)
HURRYing (but: hurried; hurries)

imaginARY
IMMENSEly
incidentALLY
incredIBLE
inDEPENDENT (independence)
instantanEous
irRESISTible
IsrAEl

JEWELry
JUDGment

LEIsure
LIBRary (LIBRarian)
LIKELIhood (from: likely)
loneLIness (from: lonely)
lovABLE

MANAGEment
maTHEMatics
MEDICine
misCHIEF
misCHIEVOUS
misSPELL

neCESSary (necessarily)
nEITHER
nIEce
NINEty (but; NINth)
NOTICEable

oCCasion
oCCur (but: occurrence; occurring)
oMITTed (but: omit)
outRAGEous

PAStime
PEACEable
PERSONally (referring to a person)
perSONNel (referring to a group, crew)
PHYSICian
pleasANT
poSSeSS (and: possessed; possessing)
potaTOES
practICE
preCEDing (and: preCEDent)
preJUDice
priVILege
proFESS (and: professor; professing)
purSUIT

reCEIPT (and: receive)
reCOGnize (and reCOGnition)
reCOMMEND
REFERence (but: referring)
REQUIREment
RESPECTIVEly
RIDiculous

SAFEty
SCARCEly
SCENEry
SCHEdule

secREtary
SEIZE
sePARate
SERGEant
SEVEREly
SHINing (from: shine)
shRIEK
SIEGE
simiLAR
sinCEREly
SOUvenir
statue (a monument)
staTUTE (a law)
STOPped (from: stop)
STUDYing (but: studied; studies)
sucCEED
suddenNESS
SURely
SURprise
SWIMming

TELEvision
temperATURE (temperate)
tomaTOES

toMORROW
TRACEable
tRAGEdy
tresPASSing
TRULY (but: true)

UMBRella
unDOUBTedly
unFORTUNATEly
unNECESSARY
USage

VEGEtable
vilLAIN

WEDnesday
WEIGH
WIELD
woMAN (one female)
woMEN (more than one female)
WRITing (from: write)
WRITTEN
YIELD

Somewhat More Difficult Words

abunDANCE
aCCoMModate
acquaintANCE
advantAGEous
advisABLE
AFFECTIONATEly
aPOLOgize
apPARENT
apPETite
approxiMATEly
ARCtic
auxiLIARy

BACHelor
balANCE
bankRUPTcy
barGAIN
begGAR
BENEfit
BIcycle
boundARY
BriTAIN
burGLAR

calendAR

SPELLING

canCELLation
caRAMel
CARRIage (but: carrying)
CAVALry (horse soldiers)
cenSUS
CEILing
cEmEtEry
CHANGEable (but: changing)
colOR
colUMN
comMISSION
comMITTee
comPARAtive
comPETent
conCEIT
conGRATulations
CONNECTicut
contagIous
conVENient
corPORal (the soldier)
corPOREal (bodily)
counterFEIT
CRITICize
curIOSity (but: curious)

DEcisively
disAPPEAR
disAPPOINT
disSATISFY
disSOLVE
drunkenNESS

EIGHTH
envIRONment
exCEEDING
EXCITEment
exerCISE

FORbid

forcIBLY
FOREman
FOREsee
FREIGHT

gAUge
GRIEvance
GUArantee

ilLEGIBLE
ilLITERATE
ilLOGICAL
IMminent (about to happen)
inflaMMable
INTERpret
irrePARable

LABORatory
licENSE

maintenANCE
ManhattAN
MILEage
MILLIONaire
misCELLaneous
MISSile
MOVable (from: move)

nausEous
negLIgence
nucLEUS

obediENT
OCCasionally
oCCuRRence

parALLel
paraLYsis
paviLION

permissIBLE
persistENCE
PERSONal (referring to one person)
PERSPIRation
playWRIGHT
PNEUmonia
POLLuted
proCEDure
proNUNciation (but: pronounce)
propAGanda

reCIPE (re-sip-ee)
reCUPerate
rePETition
responsIBLE
roDEOS

sanitARY
SCISSors
sensIBLE
SERVICEable
SINGEing (pronounced *dj*—means burning)

statISTics
stratEGY
stubbornNESS
suCCess
superintenDENT
superSTITIous
syLLable

torpeDOES

uniQUE
urGENT

vacUUm
VENGEance
veTOES

warrANTEE
WEIRD

ZEALous

Tricky and Hard

acKNOWLEDGment
admitTANCE
aGGreSSion
anaLYSis
anaLYZE
anNIHILate
anonYmous

BANana
BATTALion
burEAU

carBUretor

CARiCATure
CELLOphane
CincINNati
colLEAGUE
coLOSSal
coolLY
CURRiculum

DIPHTHeria
disARM
DULLy (from: dull)

ECStasy

SPELLING

grammAtical
GUERRilla
GUILLotine

HARassed
hemoRRHage
homoGENEous

icing (from: ice)
INDICTment
INoculate
inTEGrity

JEOpardize

LABELing
liQUEfy

manEUver
MASSachusetts
mayONNaise

peniCILLin
PHILIPpines
PHOSPHOrus
PICNICking
PSYCHOlogical

QUArantine
QUESTIONnaire

reNOVATE
reSUSCitation
RHYTHMicALLY

SABOTage
saCCHarine
sacriLEGE
sacriLEGIOUS
spagHETTI
SYNoNYM

tatTOO
tEnEmEnt

UKUlele

VICTuals (pronounced: vittles)

wholLY (from: whole)
wily

ZePHYR

TWO

Capitalization

PRETEST

In the space above each sentence, correct all errors in capitalization.

1. The panama canal is in panama.

2. pat's pizza palace is in the shopping center.

3. I flew on an american airlines jet when I went to california.

4. I saw the playoffs at shea stadium.

5. We received a free sample of loveli, a new soap.

6. We often quote the bible, but we don't read it often.

7. I wonder why they named that bridge the verrazano.

8. Someday I would like to visit australia and new guinea.

9. Did you know that lagos is the capital of nigeria?

10. We toured through the old section of the city of santo domingo.

11. The government plans to rebuild the south bronx.

12. The mississippi is america's busiest waterway.

13. During World War II, the german air force destroyed coventry.

24   WRITING

14. Thanksgiving day is a holiday in the united states.

15. I was amazed at the depth of lake tahoe.

CAPITALIZATION RULES

There are few rules for capitalization. Frequently we are helped by remembering what words and terms look like. Sometimes, when a word should be capitalized but is not, it looks a little naked.

RULE ONE: The first word of a sentence is capitalized:

This is true of all sentences. It is a fact we may rely on.

RULE TWO: The first word in a line of poetry is capitalized:

"Once upon a midnight dreary. . ."
"Twas the night before Christmas. . ."

RULE THREE: All proper nouns—specific names of specific people, places, and things—are capitalized:

New York City is sometimes referred to as Fun City. Before he became mayor, Ed Koch was known as Congressman Ed Koch. (Note: The word mayor is not capitalized here because it is not part of the title of the man: Mayor Ed Koch.)

EXERCISE ONE

In each of the following statements, four words are underlined. If one of the words should be capitalized or is capitalized incorrectly, blacken the right space in the answer grid. If there are no errors, blacken space 5.

1. "When Irish eyes are smilin'. . ." is a line from a popular song.
         1   2   3
      4
                              1. 1 2 3 4 5

2. There are many who like the songs of bob Dylan.
        1   2   3 4
                              2. 1 2 3 4 5

CAPITALIZATION

3. "I think that I shall never see
   ‾1   ‾2
   a poem as lovely as a tree."
   ‾3   ‾4

   3. 1 2 3 4 5

4. The mayor of Beirut rules a ruined city.
   ‾1 ‾‾‾‾‾ ‾‾‾‾‾‾   ‾‾‾‾
    1   2   3   4

   4. 1 2 3 4 5

5. Her favorite drink is coca-cola.
   ‾‾‾ ‾‾‾‾‾‾‾‾   ‾‾‾‾ ‾‾‾‾
    1   2   3   4

   5. 1 2 3 4 5

RULE FOUR: Names of geographic places are capitalized:

   the Sahara Desert, the French Alps, the Atlantic Ocean

RULE FIVE: Names of all countries, peoples of the world, languages, and religions are capitalized.

   The island of Ceylon is now known as Sri Lanka
   One of the main religions of India is Hindu.
   a French accent
   Hispanic culture
   a Roman Catholic cathedral
   a course in Russian

EXERCISE TWO

In the blanks at the right, rewrite the words from the following sentences that should be capitalized:

1. the race for mayor in new york city was an interesting one.   1. _____

2. For the first time in a long while, an incumbent mayor was defeated,   2. _____

3. ed Koch, a congressman from manhattan, decided to run for city hall.   3. _____

26 WRITING

4. it was felt that with the support of the blacks and the jew- 4. _____
ish part of the population, he would win.

5. Actually, koch got support from the midtown areas be- 5. _____
tween the hudson and east rivers.

RULE SIX: Names of city streets, special areas of a city or town, and particular areas of a country are capitalized:

> Forty-second Street (Note: Only the first part of a hyphenated word is capitalized.)
> the Loop in Chicago
> the West Side
> the Southwest
> the Northeast
> the Village in Lower Manhattan
> the South (Note: In giving directions - "Drive west" - the words *east*, *west*, *north*, and *south* are not capitalized.)

RULE SEVEN: Titles used as part of a name are capitalized:

> Mr. Rinaldi
> Dr. and Mrs. Throckmorton
> Congresswoman Holtzman
> President Carter

RULE EIGHT: Titles of honor are capitalized:

> His Honor, the Mayor
> the President of the United States
> His Excellency, the Foreign Minister

EXERCISE THREE

In the blanks at the right, rewrite the words in the following sentences that should be capitalized:

1. They drove south on the newly completed florida state 1. _____
parkway.

2. the party was being given by dr. and mrs. Grimaldi. 2. _____

3. It was an honor to be greeted by their royal majesties. 3. _____

CAPITALIZATION

4. Broadway is known throughout the world as the great white way.   4. _____

5. Many immigrants grew up on new york's lower east side.   5. _____

RULE NINE: For titles of printed material, there are certain variations:

In short titles, all words are capitalized, except words like *and*, *in*, and *with*:

War and Peace; *The Noble Savage*; *Gone with the Wind*

In long titles, only the important words are capitalized:

With Gun and Camera Through the Alimentary Canal

Note: When short words come first in the title—*The Battle of the Atlantic*—they are capitalized.

RULE TEN: Names of particular buildings and monuments are capitalized:

The World Trade Center
The Tomb of the Unknowns
Veterans' Hospital
Eiffel Tower

RULE ELEVEN: Names of special organizations and companies, and sometimes their chief products, are capitalized:

the Transit Workers Union
Exxon
Kleenex
Coca-Cola

EXERCISE FOUR

In each of the following statements, four words are underlined. If one of the words should be capitalized or is capitalized incorrectly, blacken the right space in the answer grid. If there are no errors, blacken space 5.

1. at one time, the Chrysler building was the tallest building in the world.
    1   2   3   4

1.   1   2   3   4   5

WRITING

2. The members of the UMW met with agents in the capitol.   2.   1   2   3   4   5
       1   2   3   4

3. Have you ever heard of the book *travels Through Patagonia*?   3.   1   2   3   4   5

4. This is referred to as the Bay of pigs.   4.   1   2   3   4   5

5. there has been copyright difficulty with the manufacturers of Coke.   5.   1   2   3   4   5

RULE TWELVE: In schools and colleges, course names are capitalized, but not the general subject matter area (unless it is a language):

> He studied dentistry. He took Dental Anatomy One.
> Solid Geometry Two.
> Music 101; He studied music.

RULE THIRTEEN: The first word of a direct quotation is capitalized:

> He shouted, "Fire in the hole!"

Note: When a quotation is broken by expressions like *he said*, *they called*, or *she asked*, the second part is *not* capitalized unless it is a new sentence:

> "Where," he asked, "are you going?"
> "Where are you going?" he asked. "What are you going to do?"

RULE FOURTEEN: All words referring to the Deity are capitalized:

> God created man, and man was created in His image.
> I place my trust in Him.

CAPITALIZATION

EXERCISE FIVE

In the blanks at the right, rewrite the words in the following sentences that should be capitalized:

1. "I told you," he said, "I'm taking a course in geography at mit." 1. _____

2. while taking Dental hygiene at rutgers, he met jane. 2. _____

3. The survivors said their trust in the almighty saved them. 3. _____

4. She became a specialist in higher mathematics. 4. _____

5. Despite difficulties in grammar, he did his best work in english. 5. _____

RULE FIFTEEN: All abbreviations are capitalized:

    Mr./Ms./Mrs.
    Robert Q. Cummerbund, Ph.D.
    Morris F. Moribund, M.D.

RULE SIXTEEN: The salutation of letters and the first word of the close are capitalized:

    Dear Madam: Respectfully,
    Dear Pal,   Sincerely,

EXERCISE SIX

In each of the following statements, four words are underlined. If one of the words should be capitalized or is capitalized incorrectly, blacken the right space in the answer grid. If there are no errors, blacken space 5.

1. From his <u>office</u> in the <u>Municipal</u> <u>building</u>, he phoned the the <u>president</u>.
    1   2   3
        4

    1. 1 2 3 4 5

2. The <u>latter</u> was away for a <u>holiday</u> at <u>camp</u> <u>david</u>.
       1   2   3 4

    2. 1 2 3 4 5

3. <u>Oddly enough</u>, <u>David</u> was <u>camping</u> in the <u>poconos</u>.
     1   2   3   4

    3. 1 2 3 4 5

WRITING

4. He was writing a book called New Ways to Win Elections.
          1   2   3   4

   4. 1 2 3 4 5

5. The publisher, Hall, mark, and Fame, had his contract.
            1   2   3   4

   5. 1 2 3 4 5

6. They were located in Dallas' famous golden Acre.
                        1   2   3   4

   6. 1 2 3 4 5

7. The publisher was planning to have the work translated into german.
         1   2 3   4

   7. 1 2 3 4 5

8. The publisher's son, dr. Harvard Yale was a German scholar.
                      1   2   3   4

   8. 1 2 3 4 5

9. But he was on leave in hamburg.
    1 2   3   4

   9. 1 2 3 4 5

10. He wrote a letter saying:

    Dear dad,
         1

    I'm planning to become a hamburger.
                                  2

             Your Son,
              3   4
            Harvard

    10. 1 2 3 4 5

THREE

Punctuation

PRETEST

In each of the following sentences, put in the necessary punctuation marks.

1. What a stunning flower arrangement
2. When did you hear about your exam
3. Gee I hated to hear that news
4. You have to be kidding
5. Move your chair closer to the table
6. That old house is supposed to be haunted
7. Just what did you mean by that remark
8. Great we've won the final game of the series
9. His mother said the child was lazy
10. Please come immediately
11. The address is 331 Pierson St Brooklyn N Y
12. It is nice to see you again Jack
13. Yes of course you may come to our house on Tuesday
14. That car has recently been painted hasn't it
15. You have to take the Ohio Turnpike or you will miss it

PUNCTUATION RULES

When the human race passed through the grunt and groan stage and language had been invented everyone was happy communication has been developed they said and now we can understand one another then writing was developed so that words could be given some lasting quality how wonderful everyone exclaimed now we can read and write but then they began to have difficulty understanding what was written down because everything seemed to run together how confusing they complained so they invented sentences and phrases and clauses and punctuation. "Now," they stated gleefully, "we can set our thoughts down, read them, and understand just what is meant." And that's why punctuation was born!

Terminal Punctuation

The simplest marks to understand and use are those of terminal punctuation. (These are punctuation marks to indicate the end of a sentence.) There are three of them: the PERIOD, the QUESTION MARK, and the EXCLAMATION POINT.

THE PERIOD

All sentences *that are not questions or exclamations* have a period at the end. The period is the most commonly used form of terminal punctuation. The period is also used with abbreviations:

N.Y.C., Mrs., Mr., N.J., Dr., Prof.

The period is used in mathematics: as a decimal point (3.17); to indicate percentages (25.7%); to indicate the separation between dollars and cents ($24.73).

THE QUESTION MARK

The question mark indicates the *actual words* of a question:

"What does that mean?"
"Where's our car?"

Note: Do not use the question mark for an indirect question (not the actual words):

He asked where I lived.
He wondered about it and asked me who had won.

THE EXCLAMATION POINT

This is the mark of emotion. It indicates more than usual stress on any particular word, phrase, or sentence:

> Look out!
> Watch it!
> He's dead!
> I can't believe he really did it!

There is no need to multiply the number of exclamation points used in order to show greater emotion. One is always enough!

These are marks of terminal punctuation. They cause relatively little trouble. We encounter difficulty when we meet some of the marks of *internal punctuation* (punctuation marks *inside* the sentence), particularly the COMMA.

Internal Punctuation

THE COMMA

RULE ONE: The comma is used to separate words and phrases in a series: Munson homered, bunted, walked and struck out during the game. The Concorde soared over the city, curved out over the bay, swooped low and landed at Kennedy Airport.

> In these examples, the comma is *not* used where the word *and* separates the terms. Actually, there is a choice here. If you wish to, you may use the comma before the word *and*. The only hard rule is that you must be consistent—if you use it one time, you must use it all the time.

RULE TWO: The comma is used before the conjunction that separates independent clauses in compound sentences:

> Namath hit for 12 out of 15 passes, *and* he carried the Rams to victory.
> Stabler tried three long passes, *but* he could not connect

There is one possible alternative in punctuating the compound sentence. One can use a *semicolon* instead of the comma-conjunction combination:

> Namath hit for 12 out of 15 passes; he carried the Rams to victory.
> Stabler tried three long passes; he could not connect.

If you write these sentences using *only a comma* to separate the clauses, you commit one of the major offenses against good writing—*the run-on sentence*.

WRITING

EXERCISE ONE

Place the correct punctuation—internal and terminal—in the following sentences:

1. He asked them if they had any cigarettes.

2. What was their answer.

3. They did answer but he could not understand them

4. He asked again what they had said

5. They became angry and they shouted at him

6. Why did they answer so roughly

7. They did not understand him and he could not understand them

8. How horrible

9. Misunderstanding breeds fear and fear creates hatred

10. Absolutely

EXERCISE TWO

In each of the following statements, four sections are underlined. If one of these sections contains incorrect punctuation, blacken the right space in the answer grid. If there are no errors, blacken space 5.

1. The cheerleaders seem spiritless I can see the reason why.
       1   2   3   4

   1. 1 2 3 4 5

2. Their coach has been changed several times the team has
              1   2

   lost its aggressiveness.
      3   4

   2. 1 2 3 4 5

3. He said they played poor ball that is not the real reason.
         1   2   3   4

   3. 1 2 3 4 5

PUNCTUATION 35

4. I think he has received offers from other clubs he denies   4. 1 2 3 4 5
             1   2   3
this.
   4

5. Only time will tell who is right I think I am.   5. 1 2 3 4 5
              1   2   3   4

RULE THREE: Commas are used to set off all non-essential (unnecessary) elements:

> You will, I'm sure, have noticed by now that English, while it is a language of great directness, can be, however, used to promote confusion.

Observe the preceding sentence carefully. Reread it, this time ommitting all absolutely non-essential material. What should result is:

> You will have noticed that English can be used to promote confusion.

This is the core of the sentence. The other expressions—*I'm sure, while it is a language of great directness, however*—are all non-essential. They are not necessary to the meaning of the sentence. They are all set off from the rest of the sentence by commas. They are sometimes referred to as parenthetical expressions. Visualize the commas as pairs of ice tongs poised to remove unnecessary elements. If you can remove any element *without changing the basic meaning of the sentence*, it is called non-essential and should be set off by commas. All such words and expressions—*however, of course, I think, you see*—when thrust into the middle of a sentence, are *parenthetical* in character.

RULE FOUR: Commas are used to set off nouns and expressions in direct address. When we ask a question and use the name of the person to whom we are speaking, *that name becomes a noun in direct address*:

> *Frank*, do you really want to be a singer?

or

> I don't understand, *Mr. Standish*, why don't you ask her yourself.

or

> Excuse me, *sir*, do you have the time?

RULE FIVE: If there is an unusually long introductory phrase or clause appearing before the subject of the sentence, it should be set off by a comma.

> Notice the statement of the rule itself. We have a long introductory clause before the main clause. It is, therefore, set off by a comma.

36 WRITING

RULE SIX: The comma is used to separate the day and month from the year in a date:

> May 1, 1921
> November 14, 1942

RULE SEVEN: The comma is used to separate the names of towns, cities, boroughs, states, and countries:

> Fairbanks, Alaska
> Brooklyn, New York
> New Jersey, U.S.A.

RULE EIGHT: The comma is used after the salutation in a friendly letter:

> Dear Rudi,

RULE NINE: The comma is used after the close of all letters, formal or personal:

> Sincerely yours,
> Respectfully yours,
> Your ol' buddy,

EXERCISE THREE

Place the correct punctuation—internal and terminal—in the following sentences:

1. He was I think more upset about losing than he should have been

2. Of course that's easy for me to say I have nothing to lose

3. What if you had been in the same position how would you have felt

4. Dreadful

5. Well Woody I feel that you came out pretty well

6. Humph

7. Of course the camera crew were pretty upset they always are

8. It's true however that most witnesses agree with me

9. Witnesses what do they know

10. When one fully considers all the facts November 14 1492 will be one of history's great dates

THE SEMICOLON

The semicolon is sometimes referred to as a "strong" comma or a "weak" period. Its uses are definite and limited:

1. The semicolon may be used instead of the comma-conjunction combination in a compound sentence:

    Munson singled; Jackson did the same.

2. The semicolon is used to break up a sequence or series of words or phrases:

    On the first floor he bought ties, shirts, and socks; on the second, pants, jackets, and hats; on the third, blankets, sheets, and pillows.

THE COLON

This is perhaps the most formal of punctuation marks. It is used in the salutation of formal and official correspondence:

Dear Mr. President:
Honored Madam:
My Dear Sir:

The colon is used after such expressions as *the following* and *as follows* and whenever a listing of items or reasons follows:

They saw the following: skyscrapers, ferries, bridges, and slums.
He spoke as follows: "Gentlemen!"
These are my reasons: a need for peace, a desire for compromise, an opportunity to create order.

THE QUOTATION MARK

1. Quotation marks are used to set off *direct quotations*. (This always means *the exact words used, a verbatim statement*.)

    Nathan Hale said, "I regret that I have but one life to give for my country."

Double quotation marks are used before and after *the actual words* quoted. The period goes inside the final quotation marks. Note the following:

> "I regret," said Nathan Hale, "that I have but one life to give for my country."

The quotation is split into two parts, but it is still *one* sentence. Therefore, quotation marks are around each segment of the quotation. Commas are used to set off the words that are not part of the quotation.

2. Quotation marks are used to set off special or made-up words. Occasionally one needs to use a special term, or use a term in a special way:

> He had a "neither-here-nor there" personality.
> She looked at me with a "Just who are you?" air.

3. Quotation marks may be used to indicate titles of stories, poems, or articles. (Titles of novels, plays, and books in general are usually underlined in a typescript: <u>Gone with the Wind</u>; <u>All My Sons</u>; <u>The Decline and Fall of the Roman Empire</u>.)

> Kurt Vonnegut wrote "Welcome to the Monkey House."
> Thoreau wrote "On Civil Disobedience"

4. A quotation mark within a quotation is indicated by a single quotation mark:

> The teacher said, "Nathan Hale said, 'I regret that I have but one life to give for my country.'"

The double quote shows *what the teacher said*; the single quote sets off *what Nathan Hale said*. This leads to the odd final combination of three quotation marks.

EXERCISE FOUR

Use the proper punctuation in the following sentences. Be careful to distinguish between direct and indirect quotation:

1. He said that I had said Frieda my love you are a bore

2. What I did say was that I loved Frieda more

3. You ask why I said what I did

4. I say to you now what else could I have said

5. Love can lead us to say strange things love can make us do stranger things

6. As the Good Book says Love thy neighbor as thyself

7. But what my friend if one does not love one's self very much

8. Then one goes to Shapespeare Physician heal thyself

9. Frieda said Did he not also say Throw physic to the dogs (This is tricky!)

10. Then my friend we will have healthy dogs Isn't that true

FOUR

Grammar and Usage

PRETEST

In each of the following sentences, four words or phrases are underlined. If any one is wrong, blacken the right space in the answer grid. If there is no error, blacken 5.

1. She told <u>her</u> story so <u>exciting</u> <u>that</u> the audience <u>was</u> pleased.
            1   2   3   4

   1.   1   2   3   4   5

2. They say <u>it</u> <u>is</u> you <u>who</u> <u>is</u> wrong.
             1 2   3 4

   2.   1   2   3   4   5

3. Sending a present early <u>is</u> better than <u>to run</u> the risk of <u>its</u> <u>arriving</u> late.
                               1   2

   3.   1   2   3   4   5

4. My mother <u>would</u> not <u>let</u> Beryl and <u>I</u> attend <u>the football</u> game.
                 1   2   3   4

   4.   1   2   3   4   5

5. <u>They're</u> not <u>certain</u> that <u>your's</u> is the <u>best</u> solution.
       1   2   3   4

   5.   1   2   3   4   5

6. One <u>of</u> our assistants <u>have</u> not <u>yet</u> shown <u>up</u> for work.
          1   2   3   4

   6.   1   2   3   4   5

7. Deirdre and Katrina waited breathlessly, each one hoping
          1   2   3
   she had won.
    4

   7. 1 2 3 4 5

8. It was always us kids who had to clean up after those big
      1   2   3   4
   parties.

   8. 1 2 3 4 5

9. The glove found on the field proved to be neither Mar-
                       1   2
   vin's nor her's.
        3   4

   9. 1 2 3 4 5

10. When the TV show is over, Tony knows its time to leave.
      1   2   3   4

    10. 1 2 3 4 5

11. Irregardless of what you say, you will still be held respon-
        1   2   3   4
    sible.

    11. 1 2 3 4 5

12. Margo, where is the game being held at?
           1   2   3 4

    12. 1 2 3 4 5

13. Our team consisted of Ira, Frank, Jerry and me.
      1   2   3   4

    13. 1 2 3 4 5

14. The next lesson concerned the principals of mathemati-
        1   2   3   4
    cal reasoning.

    14. 1 2 3 4 5

15. Try and forget that this one is more expensive than that
      1   2   3   4
    one.

    15. 1 2 3 4 5

16. Being that he was the only official candidate, he won the
        1   2   3
    election easily.
            4

    16. 1 2 3 4 5

GRAMMAR AND USAGE

17. If they <u>had</u> <u>really tried</u> harder, they <u>would have achieved</u> <u>their</u> goal.
        1   2   3   4

    17. 1 2 3 4 5

18. That <u>pile</u> of <u>papers</u> on the desk <u>are</u> to be filed <u>in</u> the cabinet.
         1   2   3   4

    18. 1 2 3 4 5

19. She <u>reacted</u> by <u>feeling</u> very <u>angrily</u> about <u>Linus'</u> success.
         1   2   3   4

    19. 1 2 3 4 5

20. The papers <u>reported</u> that the <u>cost</u> of <u>living</u> was <u>raising</u> again.
              1   2   3   4

    20. 1 2 3 4 5

21. <u>Among</u> the <u>doctor's</u> <u>qualities</u> was her concern for <u>others'</u>.
        1   2   3   4

    21. 1 2 3 4 5

22. The regular Friday <u>buffet</u> dinner was a <u>highly</u> popular, generally <u>excepted</u> part of the <u>club</u> program.
                            1   2
                3   4

    22. 1 2 3 4 5

23. <u>During</u> the test, he <u>wondered</u> if <u>their</u> was any <u>one</u> answer to the problem.
      1   2   3   4

    23. 1 2 3 4 5

24. <u>Seen from a distance</u>, the pond <u>appeared filled</u> with <u>cool</u> water, fish <u>and</u> frogs.
           1   2   3
             4

    24. 1 2 3 4 5

25. The pitcher <u>has the ability</u>, the desire, <u>the tenacity and</u> <u>in addition he wants</u> <u>to win</u>.
                      1   2
              3   4

    25. 1 2 3 4 5

26. The game <u>had been</u> called for darkness, <u>but</u> by then Bobby had <u>all ready</u> gone to his <u>uncle's</u>.
               1   2
            3   4

    26. 1 2 3 4 5

44   WRITING

27. The teacher said, "Both the mind, the senses and the   27. 1 2 3 4 5
                       ––––   –––––– –––
                        1   2   3
    body need exercise."
    –––– ––––
      4

28. When your sure of your knowledge, you have a feeling of   28. 1 2 3 4 5
         ––––   ––––   –––   –––––––
          1   2   3   4
    confidence.

29. On the one hand the voters disagreed with the Board, so   29. 1 2 3 4 5
    ––––––––––––––   ––––––––––––––   ––––––
          1   2   3
    they accused it of corruption.
    ––––
      4

30. The kitten cut it's paws on the broken glass of the win- 30. 1 2 3 4 5
                   ––––   –––––– ––––––––––– ––––––
                     1   2   3   4
    dow.

All communication is language. Any grunt, groan or whimper can have meaning. Simple words can carry meaning and feeling as well. But we always look for something more—greater precision of meaning, greater understanding and greater beauty of expression. And it is the tools of grammar that permit us to achieve meaning, understanding and eloquence. The rules are relatively few and generally simple—even with the various exceptions.

"In the beginning was the Word!" Not only biblically is this true. The foundation stone of language is the word. And because the word appears in many forms, it is necessary to identify it however it may be used. For us, this process of identification involves the *principal parts of speech*. A knowledge of these is no less essential to correct speech and writing than an ability to distinguish dashboard from tailgate, strike from ball, and driver from putter for the mechanic, the baseball fan and the golfer.

NOUNS

The *noun* is one of the two most important elements of our language. To prove this, let us repeat that sentence without the nouns:

The ____ is one of the two most important ____ of our ____.

What is now missing in the sentence prevents us from getting any meaning from this cluster of words. We do not know *what* we are talking *about*.

GRAMMAR AND USAGE

Definition: the *noun* is a word used to indicate a *person, place* or *thing.* Thus, within the definition itself there are the following nouns:

noun, word, person, place, thing

To be more particular, a noun names:

- a person or persons

    boy, man, angel, women, children, stars, singers

- a place or places

    city, country, beach, valleys, mountains, forest, island

- a thing or things

    desk, car, apartment, freedom*, beauty*, typewriter

Note: The nouns marked with asterisks indicate intangible, abstract things, which are no less real because they are *ideas.*

EXERCISE ONE

Circle all the nouns in the following sentences.

1. Social scientists, psychologists and philosophers claim that TV has lowered the cultural taste of our country.
2. Defenders of TV assert that the medium only reflects the choice of the people.
3. It is not their fault, the producers say, that the public likes violence and sex as entertainment.
4. War movies and police programs continue to attract millions of viewers.
5. Until a change occurs in public taste and general morals, such programs will continue to be shown in our land.

Common and Proper Nouns

Most of the nouns refer to broad categories. Such nouns are called *common nouns.*

There are other nouns called *proper nouns*. These refer only to specific persons, places or things. They are distinguished by being spelled with initial capital letters. For example:

Common Noun	**Proper Noun**
ship	*Queen Elizabeth II*
president	President Carter
house	White House
canyon	Grand Canyon

Of course, each of us lives with the most familiar of proper nouns, his or her own names:

Laura S. Goodman. William Ince. John Doe.

Gerunds

The word *hunting* seems to be some form of the verb *to hunt*. (If you are not sure what verbs are, see the section on them later in this chapter.) How do we know that it is in fact a noun? First, no *ing* form of any verb, *when used alone*, functions as a verb. Second, the word *hunting* is the *name of an activity* (thing)—like swimm*ing*, fly*ing*, drink*ing*, sleep*ing*. The rule, therefore, holds up: An activity is a thing and therefore is a noun.

Ing words that are derived from verbs and used as nouns have a technical name. They are called *gerunds*. Note the following examples:

Hunting is in season.
He likes *flying*.
Sleeping is the dog's favorite activity.
They say that *smoking* is a bad habit.
Her chief relaxation is *driving*.

EXERCISE TWO

In the following paragraph, circle all the common nouns, box all the proper nouns and underline all the gerunds.

There was a good deal of groaning at the Metropolitan Opera House Saturday afternoon when Osie Hawkins announced that Sherrill Milnes would not be singing in *Eugene Onegin*. As it turned out, the groaning was entirely unnecessary. The young baritone who substituted for Mr. Milnes turned in a marvelous performance.

PRONOUNS

Jane told Jane's friend that Jane was going to drive Jane's car to Jane's father's house.

What is wrong with that sentence? Obviously an overuse of the name *Jane*. Using a *pronoun*—a word used in place of a noun—you could rewrite the sentence as follows:

Jane told *her* friend that *she* was going to drive *her* car to *her* father's house.

Antecedents

The second sentence about Jane is much improved over the first. But it also illustrates some of the difficulties in using pronouns. When we say "her car," do we mean Jane's car or her friend's car? Probably Jane's, but, as the saying goes, "If it *can* be misunderstood, it *will* be misunderstood!" The difficulty we have here arises from *indefiniteness of antecedent*. An antecedent is the word to which a pronoun refers.

In a well-constructed sentence, a pronoun has only one possible antecedent. In our sentence, there are two. The problem can be cleared up if Jane's friend is male:

Jane told her friend Tom that she was going . . . .

If Jane's friend is female, you might try something like this:

To her friend, Jane said that she was going . . . .

Here there is no misleading noun between Jane and the pronouns which refer to her.

Agreement: Now let us look at some of the rules for substituting pronouns for nouns.

RULE ONE: There *must be* agreement in gender (*sex*) *between the noun and the pronoun that takes its place.*

Noun	Pronoun
man (male star)	he-his-him (male stand-in)
woman (female star)	she-her(s)-her (female stand-in)
car (any neuter object)	it-its-it (neuter stand-in)

RULE TWO: *There must be* agreement in number.

Noun	Pronoun
boy (singular)	he-his-him (singular)
boys (plural)	they-their(s)-them (plural)
girls (plural)	they-their(s)-them (plural)
cars (plural)	they-their(s)-them (plural)

Note: In the plural, there is no distinction among male, female, and neuter forms of the pronoun.

RULE THREE: *There must be* agreement in case.

	Noun	Pronoun
1.	The *man* works.	*He* works. (This is the *subjective case: Man* is the performer of the action.)
2.	The car hit the *man*.	The car hit *him*. (This is the *objective case: Man* receives the action of the verb.)
3.	This is the *man's* hat.	This is *his* hat. (This is the *possessive case: His* indicates ownership.)

Singular Noun	Pronoun (Nominative)	Pronoun (Objective)	Pronoun (Possessive)
man (masculine)	he	him	his
woman (feminine)	she	her	her(s)
chair (neuter—neither masculine nor feminine)	it	it	its

Plural Noun			
kings (masculine)	they	them	their(s)
girls (feminine)	they	them	their(s)
cars (neuter)	they	them	their(s)

If you have a good ear for the English language, you may be able to determine the correct pronoun just by listening to what sounds right. For example, suppose you were asked to substitute the correct pronoun in the following sentence:

Mother drives a car.

If you can tell that the correct sentence is, "She drives a car," rather than "Her drives a car," you are probably among those who can profitably move through this section quickly.

Here is another example. In the following sentence, substitute a pronoun for the italicized word:

Ship the *machines* to Seattle.

The correct pronoun is *them*. "Ship *them* to Seattle," not "Ship *they* to Seattle."

Possessive Pronouns

There is one group of specialized pronouns which sometimes causes trouble. These are the *possessive pronouns*. Except for *mine*, they all end with *s*, and they *never* take an apostrophe. NEVER! Here they are:

mine, his, hers, yours, ours, theirs, its

Use possessive pronouns in the following way:

The house was *Yolanda's*. The car was *Jose's*.
The house was *hers*. The car was *his*.

Alvin and Lynnette's house.
Their house.

EXERCISE THREE

On the lines provided, rewrite the following sentences, using pronouns.

1. Paul told Paul's father, Steve, that Steve ought to play golf.

2. Steve explained that Paul's father could not play golf.

3. Steve's wife told Steve's wife's husband that Steve and Steve's son should both play golf on Sundays, so that Steve's wife could have some peace.

_____

_____

A common problem involving the use of pronouns arises in compound forms. For example:

(Mary and I, Mary and me) are classmates.
(He and I, Him and me) are on the team.

The rule is that each pronoun has to be in the same case as the other compound element. For example, if one element is in the subject form, the other must be in the subject form, too. Thus:

Mary and *I* are classmates.
He and *I* are on the team.

All these pronouns are used as subjects. A simple test of their correctness is to handle each pronoun separately:

(I, Me) am a classmate.

You would say *I* am a classmate.

Here is another example:

The teacher scolded (Frank and I, Frank and me).

What is called for here is the *object form*—receiving the action of the verb. Therefore:

The teacher scolded Frank and *me*.

Again, you could drop the word *Frank* and try it simply with:

The teacher scolded (I, me).

The answer is: The teacher scolded *me*.

EXERCISE FOUR

In the following sentences, circle the correct pronouns.

1. They offered Donald and (I, me) a ride to town.

2. (Donald and I, Donald and me) refused.

3. Then (him, he) and Timmy drove off.

4. We noticed that (Timmy and him, Timmy and he) were angry.

Who and Whom

The two pronouns that give people the most trouble are *who* (*whoever*) and *whom* (*whomever*). There are simple rules for the use of these pronouns.

If you can substitute the pronoun *I, he, she we,* or *they,* use the relative pronoun *who.*

If you can substitute the pronoun *me, him, her, us,* or *them,* use the relative pronoun *whom.*

Let us test this procedure:

To (whom, who) should I give it?

Would you say,

Should I give it to *he*?

or

Should I give it to *him*?

You would say "to *him.*" Therefore:

To *whom* should I give it?

One more example:

(Whom, who) told you that?

Make the same test. One would not say,

Her told me that.

or

Him told me that.

Therefore, the answer is,

Who told you that?

The less complicated we make this, the easier it is to grasp. Make use of the rules and the sound in handling these problems. Observe how, even in slightly more complex sentences, the rule still applies:

The MP's caught the soldier (who, whom) they thought was a deserter.

Apply the rule:

>They thought (he, him) was a deserter.
>They thought *he* was a deserter.

Therefore:

>The MP's caught the soldier *who* they thought was a deserter.
>
>Give the award to (whoever, whomever) you want.
>You want to give it to (he, him).
>You want to give it to *him*.

Therefore:

>Give the award to *whomever* you want.

Pronouns and Gerunds

There is one hard and fast rule concerning the use of pronouns with the gerund: *Always use the possessive form of the pronoun before a gerund.* Thus:

>They objected to *my playing* the drums late at night.
>I could not stand *her talking* all the time.

It is *always incorrect* to say,

>We objected to *them* sitting on the stoop.

or

>He inspired *them* running for office.

EXERCISE FIVE

In the following sentences, choose between who, whoever, whom *or* whomever. *Circle the correct answer.*

1. He spoke to (whoever, whomever) was willing to listen.

2. (Who, Whom) did you say taught you how to throw a pass?

3. Where did you go, and to (who, whom) did you speak?

4. (Who, Whom) shall I say called you?

5. I don't care (who, whom) you tell about it.

GRAMMAR AND USAGE

6. The men and women (who, whom) have been elected are quite honest.

7. (Whoever, Whomever) laughs last usually laughs best.

8. For (who, whom) did you vote?

9. Do you know anyone (who, whom) can keep a secret?

10. I have no idea as to (whom, who) will be chosen.

EXERCISE SIX

Circle the pronouns in the following sentences.

1. The star of a current Broadway hit said that she was disturbed by audience reaction to her play.

2. Many members of the audience showed their enthusiasm by jumping onto the stage and joining her.

3. They also showed their bad manners by raising their voices and shouting at her from their seats.

4. This has led the producer to stop his policy of audience participation.

5. "It is unfortunate," he said, "but I must protect her, myself and the theater from these people."

EXERCISE SEVEN

In the blanks at the right, fill in the missing pronouns.

1. The replacement for Farrah will find (?) shoes difficult to fill.   1. _____

2. Ships are often regarded as feminine. Speaking of the old carrier *Saratoga*, crew members said, "(?) is a good ship."   2. _____

54   WRITING

3. With the advent of the jet, the propeller plane has lost (?)   3. _____
    place in transatlantic travel.

4. The team won (?) second World Series title in a row.   4. _____

5. Going up the hill the car lost (?) power.   5. _____

6. Secretariat and Affirmed are tied in (?) bid for fame.   6. _____

7. The spectators roared (?) approval.   7. _____

8. Sarah rode the best race of (?) career.   8. _____

9. The woman jockeys won (?) places on the circuit.   9. _____

10. Howard replied to (?) critics that (?) was here to stay.   10. _____

EXERCISE EIGHT

In the blanks at the right, fill in the missing pronouns.

The team was proud to have a woman as coach. When (1)   1. _____
shouted, (2) jumped. After (3) first loss, (4) nearly skinned (5)   2. _____
alive. (6) looked at (7) as though (8) hated (9). Actually, (10)   3. _____
would have given a hard time to anyone who dared to say a   4. _____
harsh word about (11).   5. _____
                                                                     6. _____
                                                                     7. _____
                                                                     8. _____
                                                                     9. _____
                                                                     10. _____
                                                                     11. _____

VERBS

We have stated that the noun is one of the two most important parts of speech. *The other member of this powerful duo is the verb.* Let us repeat the first sentence of this paragraph, this time without the verbs:

GRAMMAR AND USAGE

We _____ that the noun _____ one of the two most important parts of speech.

Here we have bulk but no motion—a train with no engine. If the noun provides the body, the verb provides the heart.

Definition: What, specifically, do we mean by a *verb?* The verb is the word which *designates action* or *indicates a state of being.* This is merely a way of saying that everything either *does* or *is* something.

Verb of Action

Action can be physical or mental. If *run, jump, fly* and *hit* represent action, so do *think, ponder, muse* and *dream.* An action of any sort is indicated by a *verb.*

State-of-Being Verb

Another name of a *state-of-being verb* is *linking verb.* Such a verb reveals no action; it states that something simply exists. The English verb used for this is *to be.* Why is this verb called a "linking" verb?

It *is* a verb.

Notice in this sentence that while no action is performed, a relationship is established between *it* and *verb.* The nature of that relationship is provided by the verb *is.*

There are other linking verbs besides *to be:*

The flower *smells* sweet.
Your car *seems* undamaged.
You *look* well.

Each of these verbs—*smells, seems, look*—is basically a word denoting action. But in the sentences above no action is involved: the rose is not *doing* the *smelling,* nor is the car *seeming* anything, nor are you *doing any looking.* Once again, then, we have the *verbs* as linking words, even though they are not part of the verb *to be.* A sure test for this is to substitute some form of the verb *to be.* Thus:

The flower *smells* sweet.—The flower *is* sweet.
Your car *seems* undamaged.—Your car *is* undamaged.
You *look* well.—You *are* well.

EXERCISE NINE

In the blanks at the right, indicate whether the italicized verbs in each sentence are action verbs or state-of-being verbs.

1. It *comes* as no surprise *to observe* that airline patrons *are* concerned.   1. _____

2. International "skyjacking" *is* all too common.   2. _____

3. At one time, a person *could fly* in relative security and calm.   3. _____

4. Now, however, all of us *are* somewhat nervous.   4. _____

5. What *seemed* to be the easiest form of transportation, now, *is* not so secure.   5. _____

Verb Tense

Let us spend a little time now considering the matter of verb *tense*. It is through verb tense that the time of an action is indicated.

Before we can look at verb tenses, we must know something about the principal parts of verbs. Each verb has three principal parts: *present, past, past participle*. The past participle is always formed with the use of *have, has* or *had* as an auxiliary or helping verb. Here is an example of three chief parts of the verb *to help*:

Singular

Present	I help
Past	I helped
Past Participle	I have helped
	I had helped

The verb *to help* is an example of a *regular verb*. The past and the past participle forms are achieved by the simple addition of *ed*. For many verbs only the *d* is added:

smile-smiled-smiled
struggle-struggled-struggled.

GRAMMAR AND USAGE

There are also many verbs which are *irregular* in form. To learn these irregular verbs thoroughly is really a matter of memorizing, visualizing and using.

Here is a list of frequently troublesome irregular verbs:

Present	Past	Past Participle (have, has, had)
arise	arose	arisen
bear (to carry)	bore	borne
become	became	become
begin	began	begun
bite	bit	bitten
blow	blew	blown
break	broke	broken
bring	brought	brought
burst	burst	burst
choose	chose	chosen
come	came	come
dive	dived (dove)	dived
do	did	done
draw	drew	drawn
drink	drank	drunk
drive	drove	driven
eat	ate	eaten
fall	fell	fallen
fly	flew	flown
forget	forgot	forgotten
freeze	froze	frozen
get	got	gotten
give	gave	given
go	went	gone
grow	grew	grown
hang (picture, object)	hung	hung
hang (a person)	hanged	hanged, hung
hide	hid	hidden
hold	held	held
know	knew	known
lay (to put)	laid	laid
lead (to guide)	led	led
lend	lent	lent
lie (to recline, to be horizontal)	lay	lain
lie (to tell an untruth)	lied	lied
ride	rode	ridden
ring	rang	rung
rise	rose	risen
run	ran	run
shake	shook	shaken

shine (sun, moon)	shone	shone
shine (shoes)	shined	shined
show	showed	showed, shown
shrink	shrank	shrunk, shrunken
sing	sang	sung
sink	sank	sunk
sit	sat	sat
speak	spoke	spoken
steal	stole	stolen
swim	swam	swum
take	took	taken
teach	taught	taught
tear (to rip)	tore	torn
throw	threw	thrown
wake	woke, waked	waked, woken
wear	wore	worn
write	wrote	written

EXERCISE TEN

Fill in the missing principal parts of the following verbs.

	Present	Past	Past Participle
1.	grow	_____	_____
2.	_____	rose	_____
3.	_____	_____	lain
4.	_____	lied	_____
5.	throw	_____	_____
6.	_____	burst	_____
7.	_____	_____	waked, woken
8.	_____	lent	_____
9.	fly	_____	_____
10.	_____	bore	_____

There are five particularly important tenses in our language: *present, past, present perfect, past perfect* and *future*.

The Present: This tense has two main functions: to indicate action or state of being at the present time and to show an action or state of being that is characteristically true.

>Where are you? I *am* here. (present time)
>What do you always do after a game? I *take* a shower. (characteristically true)

To show action that is taking place *as you speak*, use the *present continuous tense*. This tense is formed by adding a helping verb—*is, are, am*—to the *ing* form of the verb.

>What are you doing? I *am writing* a book.

The Past: This tense indicates an action or condition which took place or existed at a definite *time* in the past. Often, this time is specifically stated.

>I *saw* him *yesterday*.
>I *spoke* to them *last year*.
>I *spoke* to her *a minute ago*.

Sometimes, the time is not specifically stated. We learn of it through other clues in the sentence.

>The Roman Empire *fell* because of its own inner corruption.

The time when Rome fell is commonly available knowledge.

The actions described in the preceding examples took varying amounts of time to complete. The fall of Rome took hundreds of years. The conversation last year may have taken only a few minutes. All these actions have this in common, however: they are definitely completed. The past tense always suggests actions that are definitely completed.

The Present Perfect: The present perfect tense is composed of *have* or *has* and the past participle. Here are two examples of the present perfect tense:

>Yvonne *has finished* her dinner.
>We *have moved* the furniture.

This is a very convenient tense. It enables us to indicate an action started in the past and carried into the present, or started in the past and just recently completed.

I *have worked* here for three months. (I am still working here.)

Past   Present

  have worked

They *have completed* the job. (We sometimes actually say," have *just* completed.")

Past   Present

have (just) completed

The Past Perfect: The past perfect tense is formed by *had* plus the past participle. This tense indicates a past action that was completed before another past action, also mentioned in the sentence, took place. For example:

She *had gone* before I *called*.

Had gone is the past perfect action. It was completed before the other action—*I called*—began.

   had gone—called

Another example:

I *had warned* him before he *took* off.

Which action place first? The warning did. Which followed? The taking off.

The Future: This is a simple tense, used to indicate something that will occur in the future. It is formed by using the present form of the verb, plus *shall* or *will:*

I shall go	We shall go
You will go	You will go
He, she, it will go	They will go

At the present time, there is no insistence on different uses of *shall* and *will*. Frequently, the word is obscured by the contraction:

I'll do it. *They'll* wait for us.

EXERCISE ELEVEN

In the blanks at the right, fill in the requested forms of the missing verbs for each of the following sentences.

1. After the pipe (?), Seymour called the plumber. (*burst, past perfect tense*)

    1. _____

2. The twins, Irene and Ann, (?) Breakstone College. (*attend, future tense*)

    2. _____

3. Hurry up! We (?) now for the baseball game. (*leave, present continuous tense*)

    3. _____

4. She (?) through the ranks to become the head of her company. *(rise, present perfect tense)*

    4. _____

5. Between seven and nine o'clock last night, the hurricane (?) his house. (*destroy, past tense*)

    5. _____

Agreement

Understanding and using verbs correctly actually involves more than knowing the tenses. There is also the matter of *agreement* of the verb with its subject.

RULE ONE: Subject and verb must agree in person and in number.

This is generally not a problem. Consider the past tense of the verb *to walk:*

	Singular	**Plural**
First Person	I walked	We walked
Second Person	You walked	You walked
Third Person	He (she, it) walked	They walked

Here the verb form is the same—*walked*—regardless of the person or the number. This is the case with the past tense of almost all verbs.

The present tense is not much more complicated. Here are the subject-verb agreements for the verb *to do.*

	Singular	**Plural**
First Person	I do	We do
Second Person	You do	You do
Third person	She (he, it) does	They do

The form differs only in the third person singular. There, *does* is used instead of *do*. Almost all verbs are the same in this respect.

>   I walk; she walks
>   I teach; he teaches
>   I sit; she sits

For one extremely important verb, agreement in person and number is a more complicated affair. This is the verb *to be*.

Present Tense

	Singular	Plural
First person	I am	We are
Second person	You are	You are
Third person	He (she, it) is	They are

Past Tense

	Singular	Plural
First person	I was	We were
Second person	You were	You were
Third person	She (he, it) was	They were

You must know all these forms of the verb *to be*. Sometimes, you will find them used alone.

>   I am.
>   You were.

Sometimes, you will find them in combination with other verbs.

>   I am talking.
>   The children are running.

In either event, you must make certain that the subject and verb agree in person and in number.

EXERCISE TWELVE

In the blanks at the right, fill in the requested forms of the missing verbs for each of the following sentences.

1. Willie (?) Tom's car many times. (*repair, present perfect tense*)   1. _____

2. The most impressive building on Fairmont Street, it (?) over every other structure. *(tower, present)*   2. _____

3. I (?) the dishes now; I do not have time to talk to you. *(wash, present continuous)*   3. _____

4. She (?) all the animals in the zoo. *(see, present perfect)*   4. _____

5. Joe (?) two pieces of cake before he sat down to dinner. *(eat, past perfect)*   5. _____

RULE TWO: Compound subjects joined by *or* or *nor* take verbs in agreement with the last subject.

> Consider the following examples:
>> Either the Hatfields or *Mr. McCoy is* going to make trouble.
>> Either Mr. McCoy or *the Hatfields are* going to make trouble.
>> Neither the bowling ball nor *the pins are* of regulation size and weight.
>> Neither the pins nor *the bowling ball is* of regulation size and weight.

RULE THREE: Compound subjects joined by *and* are always plural.

O'Hara and O'Brien *are* opening a restaurant.
The house and furniture *are* all for sale.

RULE FOUR: A number of words called *indefinite pronouns* are not clearly either singular or plural. Some of these—*anyone, everyone, no one* and *someone*—take the singular form of the verb. Some—*both, few, many* and *some*—take the plural form. Some—*all, more* and *none*—may take either, depending on the meaning.

Here is a more complete list of these words, along with the numbers of the verbs they take:

>> 1. all—singular or plural
>>   All *is* quiet. (*If the meaning is, for example,* everything is quiet.)
>>   All *are* gone. (*If the meaning is, for example,* all the people are gone.)
>> 2. another—singular
>>   Another *has* left.
>> 3. any—singular or plural
>>   Any *is* good to hear. (Any of the news.)
>>   Any *are* here. (Any of the people.)

4. anybody—singular
   If anybody *comes*, let him in.

5. anyone—singular

6. anything—singular
   Anything *goes*.

7. both—plural
   Both *are* equally skilled.

8. each—singular
   Each *is* willing to play.

9. either—singular
   Either *is* eligible for a scholarship.

10. everybody—singular
    Everybody *is* voting for her.

11. everyone—singular

12. everything—singular
    Everything *fits* into my suitcase.

13. few—plural
    Few *are* coming to the wedding.

14. many—plural
    Many *were* invited.

15. more—singular or plural
    More *is* needed. (*For example,* more food.)
    More *are* desired. (*For example,* more people.)

16. most—singular or plural
    Most *is* in his stomach. (Most of his weight.)
    Most *are* in his stomach. (Most of the peaches.)

17. much—singular
    Much *is* as it should be.

18. neither—singular
    Neither *is* good enough for me.

19. none—singular or plural
    None *is* called for. (None of your advice.)
    None *are* needed. (None of your helpers.)

20. no one—singular
    No one *is* concerned.

21. other—singular
   When the first person refused, the other was asked.
22. several—plural
   Several of the actors *are* dancers as well.
23. some—plural
   Some of them *sing*.
24. someone—singular
   Someone *is* in the kitchen with Dinah.

EXERCISE THIRTEEN

Circle the correct verb in each of the following sentences.

1. Much of her time (is/are) spent reading.
2. Either the Smiths or Mr. Moscowitz (is/are) going to babysit for Helen.
3. None of the news (is/are) good.
4. Few (match/matches) his energy and style.
5. Neither (is/are) likely to approve of your actions.

Note: Keep in mind whether these words are singular or plural when determining the number of possessive pronouns that follow them. For example:

Few brought *their* lunches.

Both *few* and *their* are plural.

Everybody should bring *his* own lunch.

Both *everybody* and *his* are singular.

EXERCISE FOURTEEN

In the blanks at the right, fill in the requested forms of the missing verbs for each of the following sentences.

1. When they sang, I noticed that they (?) up the words.   1. _____
   (mix, past perfect tense)
2. They say she (?) working here. (*begin, present perfect*   2. _____
   tense)

3. I don't know when he (?). (*leave, future tense*)   3. _____
4. Our clothes were soaking, so we (?) them out. (*wring, past tense*)   4. _____
5. He (?) them up. (*shake, past perfect tense*)   5. _____
6. Because they ride so well, they (?) me. (*instruct, future tense*)   6. _____
7. I'm sorry, but she (?) home. (*go, present perfect tense*)   7. _____
8. You (?) badly; please don't come here again. (*act, past tense*)   8. _____
9. They (?) their father by their comments. (*irritate, past perfect tense*)   9. _____
10. The floodwaters (?) the river. (*swell, past perfect tense*)   10. _____

MODIFIERS

We have now dealt with the noun and the verb, the two most important kinds of words in our language. There are other kinds of words as well. Among them are *modifiers*—words that help clarify the meanings of nouns and verbs.

Modifiers provide color and flavor to the language. They provide for the shades of difference in expression which make language powerful, amusing, enjoyable and liveable. They are, principally, the adjective and the adverb.

Let's not just talk about these modifiers. The best way to understand them is to see them in action.

Adjectives

Adjectives are modifiers of nouns or pronouns. They tell something specific about the nouns or pronouns they accompany. They describe the word they modify. Watch:

He saw a girl.

Nothing very special in that sentence. Now:

>He saw a *beautiful* girl.

Something happens. The adjective *beautiful* tells us something about the girl.

>He saw a *tall, beautiful* girl.

The image now becomes clearer.

>He saw a *tall, beautiful, redhaired* girl.

We have a much more definite picture. From this we can establish a rule: the *adjective* modifies a noun. It describes a noun in terms of size, shape, color, texture, quality and quantity.

Note that each separate adjective *directly* modifies the noun *girl*: a *beautiful* girl; a *redhaired* girl. It is possible to have many adjectives modify any one noun or pronoun.

Most of the time the adjective appears immediately before the noun it modifies. But this may vary. The writer may shift adjectives about. For example:

>The *angry* man revealed a *furious, red* face.
>*Angry,* the man revealed a face *red* with fury.

To find the adjective related to any noun or pronoun, simply ask the questions, "How many? What kind? What color? What shape? What size? etc.," in terms of the noun or pronoun modified.

There is a situation in which the adjective is used in a unique and sometimes puzzling fashion. Look at the following sentence:

>*He is angry.*

Notice that we have a linking verb—*is*—followed by what is obviously an adjective. But the adjective appears to modify nothing. Actually, the function of the linking verb is to link the subject to another word—sometimes a noun but often an adjective—that tells something about the noun.

Study the following examples:

>The children were *happy*.
>She was *furious* about their comment.
>They were *careless*.

Note that in each case, the adjective tells us something about the subject. It *completes* the subject. For this reason, the adjective is regarded as a *complement*. Adjectives that act as complements are called *predicate adjectives*.

EXERCISE FIFTEEN

Circle the adjectives in the following sentences.

1. The gleaming, slim Concorde attracted much attention.

2. Large crowds assembled near the vast runway.

3. The great plane looked like a huge praying mantis.

4. The struts supporting the wheels were like spindly legs.

5. The surprising thing was that the plane made little noise.

6. Many people felt this was a deliberate plot.

7. They said the pilots were told to throttle down the plane.

8. But the beautiful craft won many admirers.

9. Even the harshest critics were silent.

10. Several people, however, said they would continue to protest.

Adverbs

Adverbs are adjuncts or modifiers of verbs, adjectives and other adverbs. Don't shoot! Watch closely.

Ann-Margret dances.

This is a colorless enough statement. Let us add some shading:
She dances (how?) *gracefully*.
She dances (when?) *daily*.
She dances (where?) *here*.

The *adverb*, then, gives specific information about the verb. It tells how, when, where and to what degree.

But adverbs do more than modify verbs.

She dances *very* gracefully.

We have seen that *gracefully* is an adverb modifying *dances*. The word *very* adds to the adverb *gracefully*. Thus, you have an adverb modifying another adverb.

To show how the adverb modifies an adjective, let us go back to our redhaired beauty:

The *extremely* beautiful redhaired girl entered.

Beautiful is an *adjective* modifying girl. *Extremely* is an adverb telling *how* beautiful (to what degree) the girl is.

One handy rule of thumb in recognizing adverbs is that they frequent*ly* end in *ly*. In addition, they frequently are derived from adjectives:

extreme (adjective)—extreme-ly (adverb)
strong (adjective)—strong-ly (adverb)
happy (adjective)—happ-i-ly (adverb)

Adjectives and adverbs also are capable of being varied in order to indicate changing degrees. These degrees are referred to as *positive, comparative* and *superlative*.

Adjectives:

Positive	Comparative	Superlative
hard	harder	hardest
big	bigger	biggest
lovely	lovelier	loveliest

But:

good	better	best
much	more	most
bad	worse	worst
little	less	least

The usual pattern for adjectives is to add *er* or *est* to the basic word. But many adjectives are compared through the addition of *more/most* or *less/least*:

ridiculous	less/more ridiculous	least/most ridiculous
peculiar	less/more peculiar	**least/most peculiar**
influential	less/more influential	least/most influential

Adverbs:

loudly	less/more loudly	least/most loudly
pleasantly	less/more pleasantly	least/most pleasantly
stupidly	less/more stupidly	least/most stupidly

In the comparison of adjectives and adverbs, the *comparative* degree is used when comparing two people or things: one is larg*er* than another; one is prett*ier* than another. One acts *more* reasonably than another; one dances *more* gracefully than another. The *superlative* form is used when more than two things or people are involved:

He is the strong*est* of all.
She was the loud*est* of the group.
She acted *most* graciously.
They laughed *most* uproariously.

EXERCISE SIXTEEN

In the blanks at the right, write the correct form of the indicated adjective or adverb for each sentence.

1. It is difficult to determine which of all the birds flies (gracefully).   1. _____

2. The eagle is reputed to be (strong) than the vulture.   2. _____

3. But the (high) flier of them all, according to legend, is the wren.   3. _____

4. Although it is quite (small), the wren is supposed to be (clever) than any other bird.   4. _____

5. The hawk, a powerful flier, is reputed to have the (keen) vision of all the predatory birds.   5. _____

6. And the ostrich, perhaps the (large) bird of them all, does not fly.   6. _____

7. But the latter runs (fast) than a horse.   7. _____

8. That is, it runs fast when it is not (foolishly) sticking its head in the sand.   8. _____

PHRASES

A group of words introduced by a preposition is referred to as a *prepositional phrase*. The first noun or pronoun following the preposition is referred to as the object of the preposition. A prepositional phrase works as a unit. It functions as either an adjective or an adverb.

Adjectival Phrases

When a prepositional phrase is used as an adjective—to modify a noun or pronoun—it is called an *adjectival phrase*. The entire phrase functions as one modifier:

>The sun *of early morning* is clear and bright.

Notice that the phrase *of early morning* modifies the noun *sun*. It tells "which" sun is "clear and bright."

It is used in place of the simple adjective *morning:* the *morning* sun.

Also notice that the noun *morning*, even though it appears just before the verb *is,* does not act as the subject of the verb. It is the object of the preposition. Keep this picture in mind!

>Shouting and yelling, the children *in the hallway* disturbed everyone.

Which children? "In the hallway." Therefore, we have an adjectival phrase modifying the noun *children*. The noun *hallway* is the object of the preposition *in*. Actually, the subject of the sentence is *children*. It is they who *disturbed*, not *hallway*.

Adverbial Phrases

In a similar manner, a prepositional phrase that functions as an adverb—modifying a verb, adjective or another adverb—is called an *adverbial phrase*. And once again, the noun or pronoun that follows the preposition is the object of that preposition.

>1. The fire occurred *in the laboratory*.

Where did the fire occur? *In the laboratory*—an adverbial phrase modifying the verb.

>2. The pace was too slow *for comfort*.

In this case, the adverbial phrase *for comfort* modifies the predicate adjective *slow*.

3. The plane left early *in the morning*.

Here we have the adverbial phrase modifying the adverb *early*.

Noun Phrase

A prepositional phrase, when used as a noun, is called a *noun phrase*. It may act as a subject or object:

1. *On to Richmond* was the cry!
2. He roared, *"To your posts!"*

There are two other types of phrases which may appear slightly more confusing, but they follow the same logical pattern that we have seen.

The Participial Phrase

We have seen that the *ing* form of the verb is referred to frequently as the present participle. At times, the participle may serve to introduce a phrase. Such a phrase is called a *participial phrase*. This is equally true of a phrase introduced by the *past participial* form of a verb.

Falling from a great height, the vase was completely smashed.

Here the phrase *falling from a great height* is a participial phrase modifying the noun *vase*.

The blast left him *quivering with fear*.

Quivering with fear is the participial phrase modifying the pronoun *him*.

The participial phrase is usually *adjectival* in function.

Now for the past participial form:

Stung badly, he rushed away.

The past participle of *to sting* is *have or had stung:* it is merely the main verb form itself that is used. Thus we have the participial phrase introduced by the past participle.

The Gerund Phrase

Remember that the *ing* form of the verb *used as a noun* is called a *gerund?* When the gerund introduces a group of words, the entire construction is called a *gerund phrase*, and it will be used as a noun:

Eating a hearty breakfast is important to good health.

The entire phrase acts as the subject of the verb *is*.

He loved *flying a plane*.

The gerund phrase *flying a plane* is the object of the verb *loved*.

FREQUENTLY CONFUSED WORDS

Two of the most frequently used expressions in our language are, "What I mean is" and "You know." Each of these terms indicates that the speaker is not quite sure of the meaning, is not quite certain of how to express herself, and hopes desperately that the listener does indeed understand. Usually, this is the result of confusion about words which sound alike but have different meanings, or about commonly used words whose meanings we really do not know. What follows is an annotated list of familiar words and expressions with clues to distinguishing among them.

a/an:

These are called indefinite articles. They are used as adjectives. The distinction between them is simple; use *a* before words beginning with consonants or with vowels that sound like a *y:*

a man, a plant, a usual procedure, a ewe

Use *an* before words beginning with vowels, or with initial *unvoiced* consonants:

an opera, an opening, an honest man (*but, a* history book)

accept (v)/except (prep):

For the most part, the confusion with these words stems from pronunciation. There are, however, great differences in their meaning:

Accept is a *verb* meaning to take or to receive. A sure way to recall this is to remember that a verb shows *a*ction. *A*ction begins with an *a*, and *a*ccept, the verb, is spelled with an *a*.

Except is a *preposition*. Remember the *e* in pr*e*position. It means without or omitting.

advice (n)/advise(v):

Here is a little trick. The noun *advice* means a suggestion, recommendation or guidance given. It contains within itself the noun *ice*.

Advise is a *verb* that means *to give advice* or guidance.

affect (v)/effect (n):

Affect is a *verb* meaning to have an influence upon, to cause, to assume an attitude. Remember — *a*ction (v) — *a* — *a*ffect.

Effect is usually used as a *noun* meaning r*e*sult. (Notice the *e*.) Remember the expression *cause and effect*.

aggravate (v)/irritate (v):

Here are two of the most wanted items in the lists of *mis*usage! Colloquial use, TV advertising and general sloppiness cause the difficulty.

Aggravate is a *verb* meaning *to make worse, to intensify*. To aggravate a situation means to make a bad situation even worse:

> The problems of achieving peace are *aggravated* by the actions of terrorists.

Irritate is a *verb* which means *to annoy, to pester, to provoke, to exasperate:*

> Crying children will *irritate* a busy, harassed mother; a hungry husband demanding dinner will surely *aggravate* her condition.

all right:

Here is a strange contradiction: we are asked to spell one word, and we must respond with two. But that's the clue: *all* right — two *l*'s, two words.

GRAMMAR AND USAGE

The other words of this group have only one *l* and are only one word:

almighty, almost, already, although, altogether, always

alley (n)/ally (n, v):

Alley is a *noun* (pronounced al-ee). It rhymes with Sally. Its plural —REMEMBER THE RULE!—is simply alleys.

Ally is both a *noun* and *verb* (pronounced al-lie). As a noun, it means a companion, friend or partner; as a verb, it means to become a companion or partner. Its plural is spelled al*lies*.

allusion (n)/illusion (n):

Allusion means a reference to, a hint. It comes from the verb *to allude to*.

Illusion means a false impression or a mistaken notion. Thus, a little earlier we made an *allusion* to Nathan Hale; in a desert we may see a mirage, an optical *illusion*.

altar (n)/alter (v):

Here it is the similarity of pronunciation which causes difficulty:

Altar is a *noun* meaning a platform or raised table related to worship or s*a*crifice. (Keep the *a* in mind.)

Alter, the *verb*, means to change or to revise.

amount (n, v)/number (n, v):

Each of these refers to the same general idea.

Amount is the noun which refers to a *mass* of some one thing: She always carried a small *amount* of money. There is a tremendous *amount* of power in the Oakland Raiders' offensive line.

Number is the noun which refers to *many individual units:* There were a *number* of fumbles during the game. He had a *number* of coins in his hand.

When we use *number*, we use a plural noun when called for: *a number of coins;* a *number* of beautiful *women.* The term *amount* is tied to the singular: an *amount* of *power, beauty, wealth.*

as (conj)/like (prep):

As is a *subordinating conjunction* which introduces a dependent element and shows comparison. In all cases where a verb does or can follow, use *as:* Do *as I do.* He speaks *as I do.* He is *as tall as I* (am).

Like is a preposition, and it *must* be followed by a noun or pronoun in the objective case: He speaks *like me.* Act *like her.* It sounded *like a mob.*
The test is simple: if you can add a verb after the comparison, use *as;* if not, use *like.*

ascent (n)/assent (n, v):

Ascent is a *noun* meaning the act of going up, of rising: Hillary made the *ascent* of Mount Everest. Here is a trick: break the word into two parts—a-scent: scent is an odor; an odor rises—hence, ascent—going up, rising.

Assent, the *noun,* means approval. The verb *to assent* means to give approval.

bare (adj, v)/ bear (v)/ bear (n):

Bare: Something which stands exposed or uncovered is *bare* (adj). To remove one's hat is *to bare* (verb) one's head. As a verb, *bare* has the following principal parts: bare; *bared* (past); have, has, had *bared.*

Bear: To carry something or to withstand pain is *to bear* (verb) it: Grin and *bear* it! The principal parts of the verb are bear; *bore* (past); have, has, had *borne.*

Bear: The great hairy creature, brown, black or white, is called a *bear* (noun): I'm so hungry I could eat a *bear!*

bazaar (n)/bizarre (adj):

A *bazaar* is a marketplace.

Bizarre is an adjective meaning exotic, out of the ordinary, strange: He visited a *bizarre bazaar* in the Casbah.

been (v):

Been is the past participle of the verb *to be*. It is *always* used with a helping verb: *I have been* there. He *has been* there. *They've* all *been* there. *(They've* is a contraction for *they have.)*

being (n, v):

Being, the *noun*, means a person or creature: He is a sensible *being*.

Being is the present participle of the verb *to be*. As such it may introduce a participial phrase: *Being a good citizen,* she pays her taxes cheerfully.

Being is *never* used to introduce a dependent clause: *Being he was hungry,* he ate.

Even worse is: *Being that* he was hungry, he ate.

NEVER USE THE EXPRESSIONS *being he* or *being that he* . . . .

The correct forms are *Since* he was hungry . . . or *Because* he . . . .

beside (prep)/besides (adv):

Beside as a *preposition* introduces a phrase. The first noun or pronoun that follows it is its *object. Beside* means alongside of, next to: The spider sat down *beside* her. Park the car *beside* the house.

Besides is an adverb that means in addition to, also: He is a good punter, *besides* being a good passer.

breathe (v)/breath (n):

The verb *to breathe* (pronounced breethe) means to draw *breath* (noun)—pronounced breth.

bring (v)/take (v):

To bring means movement *towards* the speaker.
To take means movement away from the speaker.

WRITING

Remember: Bring it here! Take it away!

burst (n, v)/bust (n):

The noun *burst* means the sudden explosion itself: A *burst* of flame soared skyward. To *burst* means to shatter explosively and suddenly. The principal parts of the verb are burst; *burst* (past); have, has had *burst*.

Bust is a noun which means a portrait or piece of sculpture, or that part of the human body between the waist and head.

The contemporary colloquial TV and headline use of the word *bust* to mean a raid is exactly that—colloquial, TV-ese, journalese—and not grammatically correct!

Calvary (n)/cavalry (n):

The problem here is just sloppy pronunciation. The term *Calvary* refers to the place of the Crucifixion. It is pronounced Cal-va-ry.

Cavalry means horse soldiers and is pronounced cav-al-ry. Think of the French *cheval* or the Spanish *caballo*.

EXERCISE SEVENTEEN

Circle the correct word in each of the following sentences.

1. He was unwilling to (accept, except) my gift.
2. I had bought it in a Moroccan (bazaar, bizarre).
3. It was really my (advice, advise) that changed his mind.
4. And that in itself was a rather (bazaar, bizarre) matter.
5. It is usually very difficult to (advice, advise) him about anything.
6. But since he was annoyed, all I said only served to (aggravate, irritate) him.
7. Actually, I had made absolutely no (illusion, allusion) to his attitude.
8. Even that admission did little to (altar, alter) his opinion.
9. I had spoken to him any (amount, number) of times.
10. If he continues this way, he will (burst, bust) with frustration.

11. I (been, have been) there often.
12. This sensitivity was something he had had to (bear, bare) since childhood.
13. (Being, Being that, Because) he was my friend, I tried to understand.
14. From inside, he ordered them to (take, bring) the boxes from the yard to him.
15. But he did say he would speak to no one (accept, except) me.

capital (adj, n)/ capitol (n):

Capital—*a*djective—m*a*in, princip*a*l, chief—remember the *a*'s. As a noun, *capital* means wealth or money:capital and labor. It also means a large letter in print, or the principal city in a state or nation: Washington, D.C. is the capital of the U.S.A.

Capitol—noun—is a specific g*o*vernment building, frequently with a d*o*me. Visualize the capit*o*l d*o*me in Washington, D.C.

Note: Capit*o*l with an *o* is used *only as a noun*. Capit*a*l spelled with *a* may be an *adjective* or *noun*, depending upon its use.

coarse (adj)/course (n):

Coarse as an *adjective* means rough, unrefined and may be applied to salt, sugar or people. Visualize: co*a*rse—*a*djective.

Course is a *noun* which means a r*oute* or direction, or a r*out*ine state of things, like a c*our*se of study.

complement (n, v)/compliment (n,v):

Complement is a *noun* meaning a crew or staff, or anything which completes something: the ship's complement.

As a verb, *complement* means to bring to completion.

Compliment as a noun or verb means either praise or applause given, or to praise or applaud.

comprise (v)/consist of (v):

To *comprise* means to be made up of. Note its particular use: A football team *comprises* eleven men.

Consist of also means to be made up of. However it is always followed by *of:* A football team *consists of* eleven men.

conscience (n)/conscious (adj):

Conscience is pronounced con-shens. Think of con-*science:* Jimminy Cricket was his conscience.

Conscious, the adjective, is pronounced con-shus: He was still conscious after his fall.

consul (n)/council (n)/counsel (n,v):

A *consul,* pronounced kon-sul, is a diplomatic representative.

A *council,* pronounced cown-sil, is an advisory body.

Counsel, pronounced cown-sil, as a noun means the advice or suggestion given. As a verb, it means to advise, to suggest.

continual (adj)/continuous (adj):

(Note the *al* and *ous* — typical adjective endings.)

Continual: Visualize a faucet not quite shut. The water comes out in a long line of *separate, individual drops*—this is a *continual* flow. Open the tap a little more. Now you have a thin, *unbroken* flow of water—it is *continuous.* A *continuous* noise never stops; a *continual* noise is constantly repeated.

could of/would of/should of:

These are three completely wrong expressions which should be avoided like the plague! They come as a result of pronunciation of the contractions *could've, would've* and *should've,* which are really *could have, would have,* and *should have.*

desert (n)/desert (n)/desert (v)/dessert (n):

Here pronunciation is the key.

Desert—(noun) accent on the second syllable—means worthiness of reward or punishment: He got his just *desert*.

Desert—(noun) the only one of the group with the *accent on the first syllable*—means a sandy, arid waste: The Mohave *Desert*.

Desert—(verb) accent on the second syllable—means to abandon or to leave without permission: He refused to *desert* his post.

Dessert—(noun) accent on second syllable—means the final portion of a meal, usually a sweet. Remember the term "something sweet " and you will not misspell or misuse the word!

device (n)/devise (v):

Remember *advice* and *advise*?

Device—a noun—means a tool or implement, or plan.

Devise—a verb—means to make a plan, tool or implement: You *devise* a *device*.

dye (n, v):

As a noun, this means a color added to something.

As a verb, it means to add or change a color. Note: In writing the present participle of the verb, we retain the *e:* They are *dyeing* the fabric.

EXERCISE EIGHTEEN

In each of the following sentences you must choose between two words. Fill in your choices in the blanks at the right.

1. They were (dying, dyeing) to meet the star.   1. _____

2. But he had already (desserted, deserted) the stage.   2. _____

3. He regarded giving autographs as a (capitol, capital) offense.   3. _____

4. Of (course, coarse), he enjoyed performing.   4. _____

5. It was hoped he would receive his just (deserts, desserts).   5. _____

6. But he usually refused to take anyone's (council, counsel).   6. _____

7. He was (continually, continuously) getting into trouble.   7. _____

8. Trouble never seemed to bother his (conscious, conscience).   8. _____

9. He always had a rather (coarse, course) attitude.   9. _____

emigrant (n)/immigrant (n):

This is merely a matter of direction.

Emigrant is one who *leaves* his or her country.

Immigrant is one who *enters* another country.

Thus, one *emigrates from* one land and *immigrates into* another.

envelop (v)/envelope (n):

Envelop has the accent on the second syllable—en-vel-op. It means to surround or to enclose.

Envelope has the accent on the first syllable—en-ve-lope; the last syllable is pronounced *lope*.

epitome (n):

The matter here is one of pronunciation. This word has *four* syllables—e-pit-o-me. It means the highest form of or the embodiment of something: Helen was the *epitome* of beauty.

exalt (v)/exult (v):

Exalt means to raise or to elevate. Remember the *alt* as *alt*itude.

Exult means to rejoice, to be triumphantly happy.

faint (v, n)/feint (v, n):

To faint means to lose consciousness; as a noun, to fall in a *faint*, means the loss of consciousness.

Feint, the verb, means to make a false or misleading move in order to throw someone off guard; the *feint* is the actual movement.

fair (n, adj)/fare (n, v):

The noun *fair* means a kind of open market, like a bazaar. *Fair*, the adjective, means pleasant, just, or light in complexion or color.

Fare, the noun, means payment for transportation. As a verb, *to fare* means *to go:* How did you *fare?* (get along, go). The word *farewell* means to go successfully, in peace.

formerly (adv)/formally (adv):

Form-er-ly comes from the adjective *former*, meaning prior or previous.

Form-al-ly comes from the adjective *formal*, meaning proper or suitable.

hang (v):

The correct use of this verb is a little tricky. It involves some strange human traits.

To hang a thing—picture, shelf, lamp—has the following principal parts: hang, hung (past tense), hung.

To hang a man has these principal parts: hang, hanged (past), hanged and hung.

imply (v)/infer (v):

The distinction between these two words involves a matter of direction.

Imply (verb) means to hint at, to allude, to state indirectly. It involves direction *away* from the speaker: He *implied* that I was a coward.

Infer (verb) means to draw meaning from, to grasp, to draw a conclusion from. It involves direction *towards* the person doing the inferring: I *inferred* from what she said that she was dispeased.

ingenious (adj)/ingenuous (adj):

Ingenious—with the *i*—means *i*nventive or clever. Think of the word *genius*.

Ingenuous—with the *u*—means naive, innocent, gullible.

lead (n, v)/lead (n)/led (v):

As a noun, *lead*—pronounced leed—means being ahead, going before.
Lead (noun)—pronounced led—is the metal.
To *lead* (verb) is pronounced leed; the principal parts are lead; *led* (past); have, has, had *led*.

Note: The only use of the word *led* is as the past and past participle of the verb *to lead*.

leave (n, v)/let (v):

As a noun, *leave* means a holiday or permission:

To be on leave. You have my leave to go.

The verb *to leave* means to go away from, to go out: Leave the room! Leave me alone! (This means to go away from me.)

As a verb, *to let* means to permit or to allow:

Let him alone! (Allow him to be alone in the sense of "Don't annoy him.")

lie (n,v)/lie (v)/lay (v):

The noun *lie* is the untruth itself. *To lie* as a verb means to tell an untruth. The verb has the following principal parts: lie; *lied* (past); have, has, had *lied*.

Another meaning of the verb *to lie* is to recline, to stretch out. It is very frequently followed by the adverb *down*: *To lie down*. The principal parts are lie; *lay*; have, has, had *lain*.

To lay means to put or set. *But it always takes an object—you lay something* down. Remember the old song, "Lay that pistol down, Babe!" The principal parts are lay; *laid*; have, has, had *laid*. Note:
If you can substitute the word *put, place* or *set* you should use the verb *to lay*.

loose (adj)/lose (v)/loss (n):

The adjective *loose*, meaning untied or free, is pronounced with a sharp *s*.

The verb *lose* is pronounced as though it had a *z*—looz.

The noun *loss* is pronounced with a sharp final *s*, like boss.

moral (adj, n)/morale (n):

The adjective *moral*—pronounced mor-al—means just, ethical, good. When used as a noun—with the same pronunciation—it means a lesson, something learned: the *moral* of the story.

The noun *morale*—pronounced mor-ral—means spirit, zeal, state of mind.

naval (adj)/navel (n):

Naval (adjective) means pertaining to the n*a*vy.

Navel (noun) means what is commonly referred to as the "belly button." A little crude, perhaps, but remember the *e* in b*e*lly and the *e* in nav*e*l.

obligate (v)/oblige (v):

There is a rather nice distinction between these.

Obligate means to put moral pressure on someone; to create a feeling that a favor must be returned. It is largely a psychological reaction.

Oblige has the sense of truly forcing someone to do something. Even when, as it sometimes does, it means *to please*, there is a sense of coercion.

EXERCISE NINETEEN

In each of the following sentences, you must choose between two words. Fill in your choices in the blanks at the right.

1. We were pleased by the visit of the (eminent, imminent) doctor.   1. _____
2. The vessels were lost in a (naval, navel) encounter.   2. _____
3. This has (obliged, obligated) my young brother to finish his homework.   3. _____
4. The actor had (led, lead) a glamorous life.   4. _____
5. She pleaded with her parents to (leave, let) her make her own mistakes.   5. _____
6. She felt a sense of fear (envelop, envelope) them.   6. _____
7. But I noticed that as the visit grew (eminent, imminent) the boy appeared to (loose, lose) his enthusiasm.   7. _____ _____
8. At first I thought this was a (faint, feint) to divert attention.   8. _____
9. But by the time the doctor arrived, the truth (laid, lied, lay) in another direction.   9. _____
10. During the visit, the kid was wrapped in an (envelope, envelop) of shyness.   10. _____

passed (v)/past (n, adj):

The verb is *to pass*. Its principal parts are pass; *passed*; has, have, had *passed*: He *passed* the place.

The noun or adjective referring to times gone by is *past:*
History deals with the *past:* the *past* glories of Greece.

GRAMMAR AND USAGE

peace (n)/piece (n):

The easiest way to handle these two is to master one:

Peace means quiet, or no war.

Piece means a share or part of. Think of a *piece* of *pie*.

personal (adj)/personnel (n):

The adjective *personal* refers to one's person or something private: *personal* property.

Personnel—accent on the last syllable—means a group, staff or crew: the *personnel* in the office.

principal (adj, n)/principle (n):

Principal as an adjective means main, chief, most important.

As a noun, *principal* usually refers to the chief officer of a school:
Remember: The princi*pal* is your *pal*.

As a noun, it also refers to the chief sum: the *principal* in a bank.

Principle is always a noun. It means an ethical standard or matter of belief:

It is against my *principles* to lie.

prophecy (n)/prophesy (v):

The noun *prophecy*—pronounced pro-feh-see—means a prediction.

The verb *prophesy*—pronounced pro-feh-sigh—means to make a forecast or a prediction.

The letter *q*:

The letter *q*, whenever it occurs in an English word, is *invariably* followed by a *u*.

quiet (adj, n)/quit (v)/quite (adv):

Quiet, whether used as a noun or adjective, has two syllables—kwi-et—and means silent. (On occasion it may be used as a verb, to *quiet* the class.)

Quit—pronounced kwit—means to leave a place or to stop.

Quite, the adverb—pronounced kwite—means almost, practically or somewhat.

> I'm *quite* finished. She's *quite* pretty.

rain (n, v)/reign (n, v)/rein (n, v):

Rain, as a noun or verb, refers to the moisture that comes from above. A good way to remember the spelling is to think of the lines from *My Fair Lady:*

> The *rain* in *Spain*
> Stays *mainly* in the *plain.*

Reign, as a noun or verb, means either rule or government, or to rule or to govern.

Rein (noun)—pronounced rane—is the strap used to control a horse. As a verb, it means *to control* the horse.

real (adj)/really (adv):

Here is a case of the abuse of two good words.

Real (adjective) means tangible, actual. It modifies a noun: a *real* coin; a *real* beauty; a *real* contest.

Really—the *ly* shows it is an adverb—means truly, actually. It modifies a verb, adverb or adjective and indicates degree:

> I'm *really* troubled. They *really* flew.

A good way to overcome the difficulty of choosing between them is to make use of the words "certain" and "certainly." Would you say, "I'm *certain* glad to see you"? No. Therefore, "I'm *really* glad to see you," or "I'm certain*ly* glad . . . ."

rob (v)/steal (v):

When you *rob a person or place,* you *steal* something from him or her, or it. *To rob a bank* means to take money from it; to *steal a bank* would mean to cart the whole thing away.

rout (n, v)/route (n, v):

Rout, meaning a flight in disarray (noun), or to chase an army or foe (verb), rhymes with *out*.

Route, meaning a direction (noun), or to direct (verb), is pronounced *root*.

set (v)/sit (v):

To set means to place or put.

To sit means to occupy a seat.

stationary (adj)/stationery (n):

Remember that station*ary* is an *a*djective meaning standing still.

Station*ery*, the noun, refers to pap*er*.

sure (adj)/surely (adv):

Remember real and really!
Sure, an adjective, modifies a noun: a *sure* thing.
Surely, an adverb, describes a manner: He spoke *surely*.

Remember the equation: sure-real-certain: surely-really-certainly.

teach (v)/learn (v):

You *teach* something to someone.

You *learn* something yourself, perhaps from someone else.

Teach involves giving: *learn* involves receiving.

their (pron)/there (adv)/they're (contraction for *they are*):

Their is a possessive pronoun. Remember the word *heir*, one who will inherit something.

There (adverb) means the opposite of *here*.

And *they're*, as we have seen, is the contraction for *they are*.

to (prep)/too (adv)/two (adj, n):

To (preposition) means in the direction of, or is part of all English inifinitives.

Too (adverb) indicates degree: *too* much, *too* little, *too* late.

Two, as an adjective or noun, refers to the number.

weather (n)/whether (conj):

Weather refers to the condition of the outdoors—to heat, rain, snow, and cold.

Whether refers to a relationship between two words or concepts.

EXERCISE TWENTY

In each of the following sentences, you must choose between two words. Fill in your choices in the blanks at the right.

1. Henry VIII was one of England's greatest rulers of the (passed, past).   1. _____

2. He was rarely at (piece, peace) with his wives.   2. _____

3. His (principal, principle) worry was that they were not faithful.   3. _____

4. One could almost (prophecy, prophesy) that he would behead them.   4. _____

GRAMMAR AND USAGE

5. The (personal, personnel) of his court were constantly uneasy. 5. _____

6. On (principal, principle), during his (rein, reign), there were marriages and beheadings. 6. _____
_____

7. This, naturally, disturbed the (quite, quiet) of England. 7. _____

8. The ladies of the court had much to (teach, learn) from their king. 8. _____

9. It was uncomfortable to (sit, set) on the queen's throne. 9. _____

10. The throne was frequently the start of the (route, rout) to the scaffold. 10. _____

FIVE

Sentence Structure

PRETEST

In each of the following sentences, a part is italicized. Blacken the space next to the sentence which will correct any error. If there is no error, blacken space 5—no change.

1. She had a job at the factory, *thus providing her with an an income.*

    (1) Providing her with an income, she had a job at the factory.
    (2) Her job was at the factory, thus providing her with an income.
    (3) Her job at the factory provided her with an income.
    (4) Provided with an income, her job was at the factory.
    (5) no change

    1. 1 2 3 4 5

2. *He had hoped to have received her letter by last week.*

    (1) He was hoping to have received her letter by last week.
    (2) He hopes to receive her letter next week.
    (3) He had been hoping to be receiving her letter next week.
    (4) He has hoped to have received her letter next week.
    (5) no change

    2. 1 2 3 4 5

WRITING

3. They said that *if they had had more money, they would have spent it.*

    (1) If they were to have more money, they will spend it.
    (2) If they had had more money, they will spend it.
    (3) If they had more money, they would be spending it.
    (4) If they were to have more money, they would have spent it.
    (5) no change

4. *The world famous singing group, the Beatles, honored throughout the world.*

    (1) The world famous singing group, honored throughout the world, the Beatles.
    (2) The Beatles, the world famous singing group, being honored throughout the world.
    (3) The world famous singing group, the Beatles, was honored throughout the world.
    (4) Being the Beatles, the world famous singing group, honored throughout the world.
    (5) no change

5. *After becoming a plumber, his family became prosperous.*

    (1) After he became a plumber, his family became prosperous.
    (2) Becoming prosperous after he became a plumber did his family.
    (3) After becoming a plumber, his family prospered.
    (4) His family prospered after becoming a plumber.
    (5) no change

6. *Did you ever visited at Atlanta?*

    (1) Has Atlanta ever was visited by you?
    (2) Was you ever visiting in Atlanta?
    (3) Have you ever visit Atlanta?
    (4) Have you ever visited Atlanta?
    (5) no change

7. *Her becoming angry, that was wrong.*

    (1) Her becoming angry was wrong.
    (2) That becoming angry was wrong.
    (3) It was wrong, her becoming angry.
    (4) Being that she was angry was wrong.
    (5) no change

SENTENCE STRUCTURE

8. *He said it was a long time* since he saw such a bad movie.

    (1) He said it had been a long time
    (2) He said it is a long time
    (3) He says it was a long time
    (4) It was a long time he said
    (5) no change

9. The child *is neither helpful or demanding* in his choices.

    (1) are neither helpful nor demanding
    (2) is neither helpful nor demanding
    (3) is either helpful nor demanding
    (4) is neither helpful nor demands
    (5) no change

10. The games *are entertaining and worthwhile.*

    (1) is entertaining and worthwhile
    (2) are entertaining and having value
    (3) are both entertainment and worthwhile
    (4) entertain and are worth it
    (5) no change

11. He had often asked for a date, *but I am unwilling to go out with him.*

    (1) but I am not willing to go out with him
    (2) but I have been unwilling to go out with him
    (3) but I was unwilling to go out with him
    (4) but I have no wish to go out with him
    (5) no change

12. *This pile of records are among my favorites.*

    (1) My favorites is among this pile of records.
    (2) These pile of records are among my favorites.
    (3) This pile of records contain my favorites.
    (4) This pile of records contains my favorites.
    (5) no change

13. *When among them, it is clear I am at ease.*

    (1) Among them, ease is clear for me.
    (2) When among them, I am clearly at ease.
    (3) Ease is clearly among them.
    (4) Among them ease is clearly for me.
    (5) no change

14. *Because the workers were angry, they could not do their jobs.*

    (1) Being that the workers were angry, they could not do their jobs.
    (2) Due to anger, the workers' jobs were not done.
    (3) Because they were angry, the jobs of the workers were not done.
    (4) Due to anger, the jobs of the workers were not done.
    (5) no change

15. *Did you now or were you ever a member of that gang?*

    (1) Were you ever or did you ever be
    (2) Are you ever or were you
    (3) Were you ever or are you now
    (4) Were you never or are you now
    (5) no change

16. *Obviously, they had lost there way.*

    (1) Obviously, they lost there way.
    (2) There're obviously lost.
    (3) They had lost their way obviously.
    (4) They had obviously lost their way.
    (5) no change

17. *Joe told them he had been there only once or twice before.*

    (1) Joe was there he told them once or twice before.
    (2) Joe was there before once.
    (3) Joe was once or twice there he told them.
    (4) Once or twice Joe told them he was there.
    (5) no change

18. *The building loomed above them in their car.*

    (1) Looming above them in their car was the building.
    (2) They could see the building looming above them in in their car.
    (3) In their car the building loomed above them.
    (4) From their car, they could see the building looming above them.
    (5) no change

SENTENCE STRUCTURE

19. *Being the horse of my choice, I am sure he will win.*

    (1) I am sure, being the horse of my choice, he will win.
    (2) I am sure he will win, being the horse of my choice.
    (3) He, being the horse of my choice, will surely win.
    (4) I am sure he will win the horse of my choice.
    (5) no change

20. It has been a long time *since I saw* such good playing.

    (1) since I will see
    (2) since I will have seen
    (3) since I have seen
    (4) since I had seen
    (5) no change

21. Before I left, *I have told* the boys to close the garage.

    (1) I had told
    (2) I was telling
    (3) I had been telling
    (4) I told
    (5) no change

22. *From the start, thinking as they did, are wrong.*

    (1) They, thinking from the start as they did, are wrong.
    (2) They are wrong, thinking as they did from the start.
    (3) From the start, thinking as they did, is wrong.
    (4) **From the start, thinking as they did, they were wrong.**
    (5) no change

23. *Founded in the eighteenth century, the company.*

    (1) The company, founded in the eighteenth century.
    (2) The company was founded in the eighteenth century.
    (3) The company, found in the eighteenth century.
    (4) In the eighteenth century, founded the company.
    (5) no change

WRITING

24. *Feeling it was shameful, their language was criticized by all.*   24. 1 2 3 4 5

   (1) Their language, feeling it was shameful, was criticized.
   (2) Their language was criticized shamefully by all.
   (3) Their language, feeling it was shameful, they all criticized it.
   (4) Feeling their action was shameful, they all deplored it.
   (5) no change

25. *Mark Twain, the famous American author, writing in the 1800s.*   25. 1 2 3 4 5

   (1) Mark Twain, the famous American author, wrote in the 1800s.
   (2) Mark Twain, the famous American author, written in the 1800s.
   (3) Writing in the 1800s, Mark Twain, the famous American author.
   (4) In the 1800s, the famous American author, Mark Twain.
   (5) no change

SENTENCE STRUCTURE

A sentence is a group of words that

- begins with a capital letter
- ends with a period, exclamation point, or question mark
- expresses at least one complete thought.

We talked about capitalization and punctuation in earlier chapters. Here we will concentrate on complete thoughts. One of the best ways to begin is by examining examples of incomplete thoughts:

In the summer
While he was waiting for his car
Sat under a bridge

In the summer is not a complete thought for several reasons. The first is that it does not tell you *what happened* in the summer. This is also the case with *while he was waiting for his car*. What happened while he was waiting? You are not told. In *sat under a bridge*, you know what happened. What you do not know is who sat under a bridge.

SENTENCE STRUCTURE

Each of these examples is called a *sentence fragment*—a group of words that, for one reason or another, does not form a sentence. The fragments we have been considering are not complete thoughts because they are missing something. We might make these fragments into sentences as follows:

In the summer I swim as often as possible.
While he was waiting for his car, he fell asleep.
The girl in the blue skirt sat under a bridge.

Now we have sentences. Each of these is a complete thought because it tells you, first, *what happened,* and second, *to whom it happened.*

- What happened in the first sentence is that someone swam. The person to whom it happened is *I.*

- What happened in the second sentence is that someone fell asleep. The person to whom it happened is *he.*

- What happened in the third sentence is that someone sat. The person to whom it happened is *she.*

Actually, the definition of a complete thought deals with more than what happened and to whom it happened. We will enlarge our definition after the following exercise.

EXERCISE ONE

In the blanks at the right, indicate whether each of the following items is a sentence or a sentence fragment.

1. The storm, which rained through the night.   1. _____
2. After being out in the ball park for so many hours, sitting in a cozy chair.   2. _____
3. Leroy was not happy about Susan's decision.   3. _____
4. Before Harry knew what was happening, it was over.   4. _____
5. No one, not even the owner of the car.   5. _____

SUBJECTS

We have stated that one of the key factors in a sentence is the person to whom the action happens. Another term for this is the *subject.* The subject of a sentence is the main thing about which you are talking. You will surely refer to other things as well. However, you will do so because these other things relate to your subject.

With this in mind, find the subject in the following sentence:

The woman in the blue cap screamed at the motorist.

This sentence refers to a motorist and a blue cap. It tells you that someone screamed. None of these things, however, is the subject of the sentence. The subject, rather, is *woman*. It is the woman who wears the blue cap. It is the woman who screams. And it is the motorist at whom the woman screams.

So far we have discussed only subjects that are persons. Actually, the range of subjects of conversations may also be places, things, or ideas.

My toaster has not worked for the last two weeks.

The subject here is a thing, a toaster.

Minneapolis becomes quite cold in the winter.

The subject is a place, Minneapolis.

Honesty is his greatest virtue.

The subject is honesty, an idea.

A subject, then, may be a person, a place, a thing, or an idea. In other words, the subject is a noun or a pronoun. It is not just any noun or pronoun, but the main noun or pronoun in a sentence.

To be more exact, this is what we call a *simple subject*. There is also such a thing as a *compound subject*. This is two or more simple subjects linked together by *and* or *or*.

Selma or her brother will help you with your homework.
The boys and the girls played in the game.

We can now take our discussion of subjects one step further, to complete subjects. A complete subject is a simple or compound subject, plus all the words that modify it.

The short man in the blue suit and polka-dot tie sat in the first pew.

Here *the* and *short* modify man, as does the phrase *in the blue suit and polka-dot tie*. The complete subject is *the short man in the blue suit and polka-dot tie*.

In the following sentences, the complete subjects are italicized:

India, a nation on the other side of the world, has a form of government that is similar to ours.

The last boy to be chosen for the baseball team was also the best outfielder.

EXERCISE TWO

In the following sentences, circle the simple or compound subject and underline the complete subjects.

1. My mother's visit to Africa was one of the most exciting things that ever happened to her.

2. A hard-fought victory against great odds is what he prizes most in life.

3. Lynnette and Jane sell radios, T.V.'s, and small appliances.

4. The dress in the department store window would look good on her.

5. Labels in clothing must provide certain information about how the clothing should be cleaned.

Sometimes the subject is not expressed.

> Halt!
> Get out!
> Take one and go!

Each of these statements is a command. The subject is understood to be *you*.

> You halt!
> You get out!
> You take one and go!

In formal English—and this is the kind of English that concerns us here—you may leave out the subject only if

1. the subject is understood to be *you*.
2. the statement is a command.

In other situations you must write out the subject. The following groups of words, lacking expressed subjects, are not sentences. Do not regard them as complete thoughts.

> Went to a friend's house for lunch.
> Runs 500 yards at least once a day.
> Can type faster than anyone in her class.

Up to this point we have looked only at subjects that appear at the beginning of sentences. This a common place to find subjects, but it is not the **only** place. Consider, for example, sentences that begin with *there* or *here*.

There are *thirty people* trying out for the team.
Here is *the information about fishing for trout.*
There will be *many girls* at the dance.

There and *here* can never be subjects because they are not nouns or pronouns. In the sentences just given, the complete subjects are italicized.

(Note: In sentences like these, pay special attention to noun-verb agreement. *People are. Information is.*)

Now examine the following sentences:

Will *the entire dance group* perform at the assembly?
Did *either your uncle or your aunt* call you before leaving for vacation?
Do *the members of the boy scout troop* want to go to the camp?

The subjects of these sentences are italicized. As you see, these subjects do not appear at the beginning of the sentences. This is not unusual for questions. The next questions are different. Identify their subjects:

What will happen to Rodney?
Who is going to the game?
Which is your car?

In the first sentence, *what* is the subject. Something will happen to Rodney. Because this something—the subject—is unknown to the writer, she or he uses the word *what* to describe it.

In the same way, *who* is the subject of the second sentence and *which* is the subject of the third. *What, who,* and *which* are pronouns that may be used in questions.

The pronouns *what, who,* and *which* should not be mixed up with *why, when, where,* and *how*, which are adverbs. Like the pronouns, *why, where, when,* and *how* are used to open questions. However, you must look further into such sentences to find the subject.

Why is *he* yelling so much?
When are *all our friends* going to come?
Where did *Gina* meet her date?
How do *you* expect to learn history?

In these sentences the subjects are italicized.

EXERCISE THREE

Underline the complete subjects in each of the following sentences.

1. There are paints of sixteen different colors in Estrelita's art class.
2. Will Juan, Russell's nephew, go to night school?
3. Who is going to call Rose to come to the party?
4. Why is my cousin telling those stories about you?
5. Leave this room at once!

PREDICATES

Of the two necessary parts of a sentence, the first is the subject and the second is the *predicate*.

> The mechanic *fixed*.
> The policeman *ran*.
> The car *turned*.

Fixed, *ran*, and *turned* are the predicates of their sentences. They are action verbs which tell what happened to their subjects.

The predicate is always a verb. In all the examples we have considered so far, it has been an action verb. The predicate may also be a state of being verb, a linking verb.

> The building *is* high.
> The tire *feels* soft.
> The flower *looks* beautiful.

Like subjects, predicates may be simple or compound. We have looked at simple predicates. The following are compound:

> A teacher either *passes* or *fails* students.
> Ice *melts* and *freezes* every day.
> He either *yells* or *whispers*.

As with compound subjects, compound predicates are joined by *and* or *or*.

Remember that predicates, being verbs, often consist of more than one word

She *has left*.
He *is coming*.
The music *will play*.

Sometimes a predicate will contain such helping verbs as *can*, *do*, and *may*.

She *can have* the dress in the window.
I *do believe* you.
He *may attend* the graduation.

EXERCISE FOUR

In the following sentences, circle the simple and compound predicates.

1. The company repaired every one of its cars.

2. The puppy whined and yelped throughout the washing.

3. I did call Harry last week.

4. Lu Jean was the girl in question.

5. Recently, I have spoken about the plan over and over.

OBJECTS

There must be a performer of every action mentioned by the verb, but there may also be a receiver of such action. The performer is, of course, the subject; the receiver is called the *direct object*. And it, too, will always be a noun or a pronoun. *The direct object of an action verb is the noun or pronoun which receives the action of that verb.* And such an object is always in the *objective case!*

Reggie Jackson hit the ball.

The verb *hit* transfers its action to *ball*; hence, *ball* is *the direct object of the verb*.

The clue to finding the direct object of any action verb is to ask *whom* or *what* **after the verb**:

Reggie Jackson hit *whom*? No answer.
Reggie Jackson hit *what*? He hit *the ball*.

But be careful:

> He threw wildly.
> threw whom? what?

Because there is no answer to these questions in this sentence, there is no object. (Actually, the adverb *wildly* answers the question *how in relation to the verb*.

Remember: An action verb *may have* an object, *but it does not need one*.

You will note that we have been referring to something called a *direct object*—a noun that receives the action of the verb. But there is another kind of object called the *indirect object*. Watch:

> He threw the *ball*.

Ball obviously is the direct object of the verb *threw*.

> He threw *her* the ball.

Notice that the direct object remains the same: The *ball* still receives the action. But the pronoun *her* is called the *indirect object*. It is as though we were saying, He threw the ball *to her*. And that is the mark of the indirect object. If you can put in the prepositions *to* or *for*, you have an *indirect object*.

Watch the following very carefully:

> She showed *me* around.

The pronoun *me* in this case is the direct object of the verb *showed*: showed *whom*? showed *me*.

But:

> She showed *me* the watch.

In this case, she showed *what*? The watch. *To whom* did she show that watch? To *me*. Therefore *me* is the indirect object.

Remember: If you can place the prepositions *to* or *for* between the verb and the pronoun following, you have an indirect object.

EXERCISE FIVE

In the following sentences, circle the direct objects and draw lines under indirect objects.

1. She gave them many gifts.

2. The garbage men threw them away.

3. She bought the dress.

4. The repairman sold them the radio.

5. The tackle threw him to the ground.

Now let us look at the whole sentence. The sentence is a unit containing a subject and a verb and expressing a complete thought with or without an object.

EXERCISE SIX

In the blanks at the right, indicate whether each of the following groups of words is a sentence or a sentence fragment.

1. Without which we would like to.   1. _____
2. Throughout the book, we are being taught grammar.   2. _____
3. It is not really difficult.   3. _____
4. Since when?   4. _____
5. Regardless of its problems.   5. _____
6. Study and application are necessary.   6. _____
7. Over and beyond the basic needs.   7. _____
8. Studying models of good writing will improve your style.   8. _____
9. While such current writing is not particularly grammatical.   9. _____
10. Some of it is.   10. _____

EXERCISE SEVEN

In each of the following sentences, one or more words are italicized. Indicate by writing S or O above each word whether it is a subject or an object. Remember: The noun or pronoun immediately after a preposition is the object of the preposition.

1. Leroy's *trip* to his *aunt's* was important for *him*.

2. An *experience* like this is difficult.

3. When the need is great, much *effort* is required.

4. A fine *athlete* knows the risk of *injuries*.

5. *Success* brings *happiness*; failure results in *sadness*.

6. Jerry's mother sent *cookies* for the party.

7. Juan prepared a great *feast* for his *brother*.

8. *Everyone* danced the *Hustle* with great *skill*.

9. The *search* for happiness is part of our nature.

10. Many *people* think only of their *problems*.

PREPOSITIONS

The noun, verb, adjective, and adverb may be referred to as the Big Four among parts of speech. But there are also others, which carry considerable weight. Look at the following sentence—with its blanks:

Let us look _____ the *preposition* and see just how common it is _____ our language.

The sentence makes some sense as it stands; it certainly is not precise. Do we mean "look *for* the preposition," "*at* the preposition," "*to* the preposition," "*into* the preposition"? Likewise, do we mean, "*for* our *language*," " *to our language*," "*within our language*"? The missing word is a *preposition*. Its purpose is as a linking word which establishes a relationship between two words or groups of words. Another peculiarity of the preposition is that it is always followed directly, or a word or two later, by a noun or a pronoun. The whole phrase—preposition + noun or pronoun—is called a *prepositional phrase*.

Note: The noun or pronoun that follows the preposition is always in the objective case; it is referred to as the *object of the preposition*.

Some of the most familiar prepositions are the following:

besides	of
between	to (when not used as part of the infinitive)
for	toward
in	with
into	within

EXERCISE EIGHT

Circle all the prepositions in the following sentences.

1. The maps in the book should help us to learn geography.

2. With each exercise we will reexamine our rules.

3. Studying for tests is necessary.

4. With good study habits, a student can learn new subjects in a short time.

5. Juan wanted to improve his knowledge of geography.

6. He studied each evening after work.

7. We hope to go to the country for the weekend.

8. Leroy was given a raise by his employer for his good work.

9. Lillian found the book on the shelves in the back of the library.

10. He sat between the two boys, one of whom he knew.

CONJUNCTIONS

Look back at the title of a previous chapter: "Grammar *and* Usage." The word *and* connects the two items on an equal level. You could just as easily say usage *and* grammar without any change in meaning or emphasis. The *conjunction*, then, is a linking word—a *connective*. There are three types of

SENTENCE STRUCTURE

conjunctions: *coordinating, subordinating,* and *correlative.* Here are lists of the most commonly used of each:

coordinating conjunctions:	and, but, nor, or
subordinating conjuctions:	after, although, as, because, before, if, since, until, when, whenever, where, while
correlative conjunctions:	(These are used in pairs.) both/and, either/or, neither/nor, not only/but also

A conjunction that links two items of equal importance is called a *coordinating conjunction.* The word *and* is the most common coordinating conjunction. Elements joined in this manner are called *compound constructions*: compound subject, compound object, compound verb, compound modifier, compound sentence. Let us look at some examples.

Compound Subject:

John Travolta and Marlon Brando are movie stars.

Each name is of equal importance. The names could be reversed without changing the basic meaning. The terms are *coordinate*—of equal value.

Compound Object:

Her jeans were trimmed with white and red.

Again, two equal terms are linked by *and.* We could reverse the order and we would change only the picture in your mind, not the grammatical structure. Note: Both words, white and red, are objects of the preposition *with.*

Compound Sentence:

She called, and he answered.

This sentence consists of two equal, independent parts linked by the coordinating conjunction.

Suppose now that one person performs several actions:

Muhammad Ali shouted, grinned, and clowned around.

The key point to remember is that *coordinate elements* are equal in importance; no one element depends upon the other.

There is another type of construction, however, of which we must be aware. That is when one grammatical unit cannot stand alone and is *sub-*

ordinate to or *dependent upon* another unit. To connect such elements a *subordinating conjunction* is used.

When the bell rang, the class began.

Break this sentence into two clauses: Obviously, "When the bell rang" cannot stand by itself. Think of a freight car, loaded, ready to move, its coupling device outstretched. It needs something to pull it. "The class began" is clearly independent; it makes sense by itself. Visualize this unit as the locomotive, the power unit, needing no assistance to move on its own. It is the subordinating conjunction *when* that links the two into a complete train.

Here, then, are our two types of units. The independent clause is a sentence in itself. The *dependent* or *subordinate clause* is introduced by the subordinating conjunction.

To study the problem of parallelism, examine the following sentences carefully:

1. She liked knitting, sewing, studying, and to go on long rides.
2. He was polite, thoughtful, compassionate, and to be with people.
3. Modern speedboats are smoother, stronger, and it is easier to operate them.
4. A person hoping to get an education must accept long hours of study, must give up many pleasures, and he is probably sometimes lonely.

Notice that in each of these sentences, there is a break in the rhythm of the sentence itself and an element that does not seem to fit. This comes as a result of violating the rules of *parallelism*.

Notice that in Sentence 1 we have a series of *gerunds: knitting, sewing, studying*. The use of the infinitive form *to go* breaks this pattern. The correct form would be a continuation of the sequence: *knitting, sewing, studying*, and *riding*.

In Sentence 2 we have a similar problem. We have a series of *predicate adjectives*: *polite, thoughtful, compassionate*. Again the use of the infinitive—*to be*—breaks the pattern. The sentence should read: He was *polite, thoughtful, compassionate*, and *friendly*.

Sentence 3 represents another break in the pattern: *smoother, stronger,* followed by a completely new clause. The correct form should be: *smoother, stronger*, and *easier* to operate.

SENTENCE STRUCTURE

Sentence 4 is somewhat more complex, but the same principle is involved. The correct form of this sentence is: A person hoping to get an education *must* accept long hours of study, *must* give up many pleasures, and *must* accept loneliness.

The concept of correct parallelism is easy to learn. Just let your ear and your sense of balance guide you. It becomes as easy to respond to an error of this sort as it is to recognize a break or a mistake in the rhythm of a popular tune or a familiar dance beat. If the bank threw a waltz beat into a cha-cha, everyone would respond immediately, probably by stumbling all over the place!

RULE ONE: *In order to achieve parallel structure in a sentence, balance a word with a word, a phrase with a phrase, and a clause with a clause.*

She was in favor of meeting *word with word, idea with idea,* and *blow with blow.*

Nina and Rocky showed their delight by *dancing in the morning, dancing in the afternoon,* and *dancing in the night.*

Our emotional well-being is shown by *how we look, what we say,* and *what we do.*

Leroy told Willy to take all the time he needed: *an* hour, *a* day, *a* month, or *a* year.

RULE TWO: *To make a parallel clear it is sometimes necessary to repeat a preposition, an article, or an introductory word.*

The girls went without makeup and shampoo *for* hours and sometimes *for* days.

On the test she found she could not complete *a* problem or *an* example.

He showed *that* the company had grown in value, *that* it had developed in size, and *that* it had gained in prestige in the community.

EXERCISE NINE

In the following sentences, correct the errors of parallelism on the lines provided.

1. She thought of shopping, walking along Broadway, and she felt she should visit her grandparents.

_____

_____

2. With careful choice, wise pricing, and if you are not a spendthrift you can find pre-Christmas bargains in all the stores.

_____

_____

3. Newer ideas of engineering, more skilled mechanics in service, better relations with distributors, and because they want their sales to increase make car dealers more prosperous.

_____
_____

4. The growing child wants to know why he is living, why he is cared for, why his parents are concerned about him, and to know why he must do things he dislikes.

_____
_____

5. They admired the glory of Greece, the grandeur of Rome, and they liked the traditions of England.

_____
_____

TYPES OF SENTENCES

Writing and using correct sentences will guarantee clearness and understanding. Being able to use different types of sentences will guarantee interest, pleasure, and style. It is variety in language, just as in eating, that provides relief from boredom and dullness. There are three kinds of sentences: *simple, compound,* and *complex.*

Simple Sentence

This is easy to recognize: *a subject, a verb,* and *a single complete thought or idea.*

Basketball is a great spectator sport.

Basketball is the subject. *Is* is the verb; the idea is clear and complete. But there is a chance of variety even within this narrow limit:

Julius Erving and Bill Walton are great players.

What is the subject of this sentence? *Julius Erving and Bill Walton*—two nouns connected by the conjunction *and.* They form, therefore, a *compound subject.*

Exactly the same procedure is followed when we have a *compound verb*—one person performs more than one action:

A good basketball center *runs and passes*.

Moving from this demonstration of the variety in a simple sentence, we go to the next kind of sentence—the *compound sentence*.

Compound Sentences

A compound sentence consists of two equal, independent clauses joined by a coordinating conjunction. This means, basically, that two simple sentences joined by a conjunction form one compound sentence.

The center dribbled the ball and the guard caught it.

What makes this a compound sentence? Each unit, before and after the *and*, is a complete, independent unit.

Next in order of complexity—and richness of expression—is the complex sentence.

Complex Sentences

This type of sentence consists of one principal (main or independent) clause and one or more subordinate (dependent) clauses, linked by relative pronouns or subordinating conjunctions. Keep in mind the image of a train—the independent clauses are the powerless cars. In the complex sentence, for the most part, the dependent clauses will be used as modifiers; they will, therefore, usually be *adjectival* or *adverbial* in function. One way to spot the dependent clauses wil be to notice the relative pronouns—*who, whom, what, that, which*—for adjectival clauses and the subordinating conjunctions—*when, if, since, because, where*—and others for the adverbial clauses. Watch:

The man *who painted my house* brought his ladder.
RELATIVE PRONOUN (who) + VERB (painted) = CLAUSE

Which man are we talking about? The man *who painted my house*. This clause modifies a noun. It is an *adjectival clause*.

Note: One characteristic of the relative pronoun (who) is that it introduces the subordinate clause and *acts as its subject*.

And the same design exists with the adverbial clause:

She giggled *when she saw the shoes.*

We see the subordinating conjunction *when*. The clause that follows answers the question *when?* Therefore this is an adverbial construction.

You will notice that when the order of the clauses is changed—even reversed—the principle holds:

When she saw the shoes, she giggled.

We have the same independent construction—*she giggled*—and the same subordinate (adverbial) clause—*When she saw the shoes.*

EXERCISE TEN

On the blanks at the right, identify the following sentences as Complex (Cx), Compound (Cp), or Simple (S). Be careful about compound constructions within sentences.

1. Buffer zones between wolves' territories reduce friction between neighboring packs. 1. _____

2. They also provide cover for the wolves' killings, like deer and rabbits. 2. _____

3. When deer herds are growing smaller, they find cover in these zones. 3. _____

4. Wolves seldom go into them for fear of meeting and fighting with other packs. 4. _____

5. Staying in the buffer zones the deer remain alive, and they leave to take up their normal lives elsewhere. 5. _____

6. This is part of nature's plan of survival. 6. _____

7. Man could easily learn from nature's plan. 7. _____

Sentence Variety

Richness in variety of sentence construction can be gained not only by using the various types of sentences, but also by using other grammatical forms. Observe:

She disliked washing dishes. She did it very reluctantly.

A tragic tale told in two simple, rather dull sentences. How can we spice things up a little?

Through subordination:

Because she hated washing dishes, she did it very reluctantly.

SENTENCE STRUCTURE

Here we have used an *adverbial clause* and have made a somewhat richer *complex sentence*.

Through punctuation and compounding:

She hated washing dishes; therefore, she did it very reluctantly.

Using the participle:

Hating having to wash dishes, she did it very reluctantly.

Let's try something else:

The team lost its last game. The women were very discouraged. Even the thought of "next year" didn't bring them any relief.

Because they had lost their last game, the women were very discouraged, and the usual "Wait until next year" didn't cheer them.

A compound-complex sentence brings it all together more succinctly.

Or:

Having lost their last game, the women were very discouraged; the thought of next year didn't bring them any relief.

Or:

Discouraged by the loss of their last game, the women found no relief even in the thought of next year.

As we can see, there are many ways to write sentences. In any extended writing, making choices among them will make things livelier and more interesting for both writer and reader.

MISPLACED AND DANGLING MODIFIERS

Some common sentence problems include the following:

1. Mel Allen saw Reggie Jackson hit a home run with a cast on his leg.
2. Flying low over the harbor, the Statue of Liberty could be seen clearly.

While we really understand what is meant in both these sentences, grammatically they do not make much sense. It is hardly likely that Jackson was playing with his leg in a cast; the Statue of Liberty does not really fly low or otherwise over the harbor.

Sentence 1 gives an example of what is called a *misplaced modifier*. Here the adjective phrase *with a cast on his leg* appears to modify Jackson, or even worse, *a home run*. We assume that the correct sentence should read:

Mel Allen, *with a cast on his leg,* saw Jackson hit a home run.

RULE ONE: Words, phrases, or clauses used as modifiers should be placed as near as possible to the word they modify.

Sentence 2 is a classic example of what is called a *dangling participle.* As the sentence reads now, it sounds as though the Statue of Liberty is flying low over the harbor.

One way of correcting the mistake is the following:

The plane, flying low over the harbor, came within sight of the Statue of Liberty.

It is now obvious that the plane is flying low over the harbor.

RULE TWO: A phrase or clause used as a modifier must clearly and sensibly modify one particular word in a sentence.

If the modifying phrase or clause does not observe this rule, it becomes a *dangling modifier.*

Note: The word *flying,* the *ing* form of the verb, is a present participle. It introduces what is called a *participial phrase* in the same manner that a preposition introduces a prepositional phrase. It is a modifier.

More common sentence problems: There are times when the *past participle* is used in the same way: *Concerned over his studies, his unhappiness gave him indigestion.* In this sentence, it appears that the phrase *concerned over his studies* modifies the word *unhappiness.* To correct the sentence, one might write: *Concerned over his studies, he developed indigestion.* Here the phrase modifies *he,* as it was intended to do.

EXERCISE ELEVEN

In the following sentences, there are some errors of either misplaced modifiers or dangling participles. Correct the errors only.

1. Finding the wall too high, the soldiers returned to camp.

SENTENCE STRUCTURE 117

2. Giggling all the way, the plane almost crashed.

   _____

3. Approaching the airport, the lights appeared.

   _____

4. Landing with difficulty, they jumped to the ground.

   _____

5. With the engine cut off, the crew went into a restaurant.

   _____

6. Angered by their stupidity, they approched the store's owner.

   _____

7. Annoyed by their actions, she left them.

   _____

8. They returned home, puzzled by their friends' calmness.

   _____

9. Puzzled and angered by all this, the store closed.

   _____

10. Doping, clearly, does not solve problems.

    _____

SIX

Diction and Style

PRETEST

In each of the following sentences, there is an italicized section which may contain an error in diction or style. Blacken the space corresponding to the proper correction. If there is no error, blacken space 5.

1. Because the team's manager was angry about the loss, he decided to *dump* the coach.

    (1) rub out
    (2) get rid of
    (3) remove
    (4) incarcerate
    (5) no change

2. There was *hardly nothing* he knew about the use of the tools.

    (1) hardly anything
    (2) not nothing
    (3) not hardly anything
    (4) anything
    (5) no change

3. The policeman said the suspect had been *transgressing* the law.

    (1) averting
    (2) evading
    (3) breaking
    (4) obstructing
    (5) no change

WRITING

4. *In this movie it shows* how cheese is made from milk.   4. 1 2 3 4 5

   (1) In this movie they show
   (2) In this movie it is shown
   (3) This movie shows
   (4) In this movie what is shown is
   (5) no change

5. This old *dude* could tell funny stories about his youth.   5. 1 2 3 4 5

   (1) codger
   (2) guy
   (3) coot
   (4) gentleman
   (5) no change

6. The painting was incomparable, breathtaking, exotic, and *just plain great*.   6. 1 2 3 4 5

   (1) real great
   (2) just plain extraordinary
   (3) truly extraordinary
   (4) outrageous
   (5) no change

7. Whenever she felt lonely, she turned to reading, listening to good music, and *diddling* her thumbs.   7. 1 2 3 4 5

   (1) doodling
   (2) drooling
   (3) biting
   (4) twirling
   (5) no change

8. After the fourth inning, the coach read the team the riot act, bawled out the pitcher, and encouraged the team to do its best.   8. 1 2 3 4 5

   (1) urged
   (2) extorted
   (3) coerced
   (4) wanted
   (5) no change

DICTION AND STYLE

9. The fact that she did speak with her relatives *it shows* how she feels about them.

   (1) they showed
   (2) shows
   (3) it indicates
   (4) it truly reveals
   (5) no change

10. If you fail to meet all the payments, *they will take the vacuum cleaner.*

    (1) that means they will take the vacuum cleaner
    (2) they take the vacuum cleaner
    (3) the vacuum cleaner will be taken back
    (4) it means they will take the vacuum cleaner
    (5) no change

11. The boys on the corner made such noise they *aroused the tenants' ire.*

    (1) aroused the tenants' tempers
    (2) aroused the tenants' animosity
    (3) made the tenants angry
    (4) caused the tenants' annoyance
    (5) no change

12. After being told her rights and having the law explained to her, she said, *"What's the diff?"*

    (1) "What's the row all about?"
    (2) "What's the name of the game?"
    (3) "I could care less!"
    (4) "So what?"
    (5) no change

13. She told the students to *center their attention around* these facts.

    (1) focus their attention around
    (2) center there attention on
    (3) center their attention on
    (4) center their attention about
    (5) no change

14. The President, addressing the Congress, said he was *mad*.

    (1) annoyed
    (2) with it
    (3) discourteous
    (4) in cahoots
    (5) no change

15. Ray felt that his car was *considerably different than* mine.

    (1) different to
    (2) different from
    (3) differing than
    (4) real different than
    (5) no change

16. *The movie star played her role very well.*

    (1) The movie star who was playing the lead, played her role very well.
    (2) The movie star that played the lead, played her role very well.
    (3) The movie star that was playing the lead, played her role very good.
    (4) The movie star who played the lead played her role very good.
    (5) no change

17. She claimed that she had not *robbed the money off the bank*.

    (1) stolen the money off the bank
    (2) robbed the money from the bank
    (3) stolen the money from the bank
    (4) stolen the bank
    (5) no change

18. They held many meetings about ways for *making good*.

    (1) making out good
    (2) doing good
    (3) succeeding good
    (4) making out
    (5) no change

DICTION AND STYLE

"I like this style."

What does that mean? Obviously we are referring to much more than a person's looks. "Style" involves manner, appearance, speech, dress, and all the other things which make up the total person. And just as there is style in dress, so there is style in words. People who were ever in the armed services are aware that certain speech patterns and words would not be quite suitable for most areas of civilian life. In everyday life we know that certain habits of speech and vocabulary are acceptable at work but not a home. Just as we dress differently for the movies, a ball game, a picnic, and a visit to our grandparents, so do we dress up in different levels of speech.

Note: There is a strong movement throughout our country to do away with these different levels of speech. We find people of good background and education whose language resembles what used to be called truck drivers' speech. This, however, is not really widespread; the differences in language are still with us. They certainly are for purposes of examinations!

Notice the following illustrations:

1. "Gee, thanks a million, ol' buddy."
2. "Thank you very much, madam, for your assistance."
3. "I feel deeply honored—more honored than I can fully express—for the recognition you have accorded me here."

Sentence 1 demonstrates the kind of speech we are probably most familiar with—everyday street talk. It is correct, but casual.

Sentence 2 is still quite informal, but it is a little more polite and considered.

Sentence 3 is formal indeed; it is the kind of language reserved for official and formal occasions. It is quite clear that the speaker in Sentence 3 could not respond with the statement of Sentence 1. Note particularly that there is nothing grammatically wrong in any statement. It is purely a matter of style and tone.

Not long ago, the Shah of Iran, while visiting the United States, was quoted as saying, "After *perusing* the material at hand, I decided to *give you a break*." This reflects an amusing marriage of a most formal and dignified word—*perusing*—to a widely used, colloquial, and almost slang expression—*give you a break*. Obviously, however, nobody would pour oil on these troubled stylistic waters, with prices what they are!

Here are some examples of the differences between the levels of language:

Colloquial	Informal	Formal
gabby	talkative	garrulous
take off	go	abscond
yell at	scold	reprimand

Besides knowing when to use the proper level of language, we should be aware of how to make our speech and our writing truly our own—to develop our own style. All languages have expressions which, when used properly, add color and strength. These same expressions, when overworked, become dull and uninteresting. They become clichés: "I'm hungry as a *bear*." "I could eat a *horse*." "The baby is cute as a *button*." To achieve individual style, we must be able to provide our own descriptions and reactions.

Now let us look at something else.
"How is that new hi-fi you just got?"
"Really *terrific,* man!"
"The new car in the family?"
"*Terrific!* A *fabulous* ride!"
"The movie you've just seen?"
"Absolutely *terrific*. That Burt Reynolds—*fabulous!*"
"The local pizzeria?"
"They serve a pizza, man—I mean it's out of this world—*fabulous*—but *fabulous!*"

What's this all about? Verbicide—the killing and abuse of words and language. It's not that the meaning is unclear with language such as the above; but we take powerful, meaningful words and drain them dry of meaning and power. They become meaningless. Let us, for example, look up the true meanings of the underlined words, and see if they are really the words we wanted to use:

"How is that new hi-fi you just got?"
"Really (adapted to excite great fear or dread; terrible; appalling), man."
"The new car in the family?"
"(Terrible; appalling). A (feigned, as a fable, fictitious; beyond sober belief) ride."

And so with the others—a *mythological* actor and pizza.

DICTION AND STYLE

SAMPLE EXERCISE

Study the following paragraphs carefully. Underline the words which are dull, overused, and meaningless.

Last Saturday, which was a lovely day, we took a wonderful trip. We went to visit that fabulous center of lovely buildings, fabulous displays, beautiful fountains, and wonderful things to do—Disneyland. Even though the traffic was fantastic, with a couple of terrific traffic jams on the way, it was really a lovely ride.

Once we took a wrong turn and got caught in a terrific mess. The cars were coming at us from all sides. They were blowing their horns and making a terrific racket. Luckily for us a police car came along, and he was nice enough to stop the traffic so we could turn around and get back into the line for the parking lot.

That was only the start of what turned out to be a terrific day of traveling and eating all kinds of wonderful things and seeing the absolutely great displays in that wonderful place—Disneyland.

Your list of dull, meaningless phrases and words in this exercise should look like this:

1. a *lovely* day
2. a *wonderful* trip
3. *lovely* buildings
4. *fabulous* displays
5. *fabulous* displays
6. *wonderful* things to do
7. traffic was *fantastic*
8. *terrific* traffic jams
9. a *lovely* ride
10. a *terrific* mess
11. a *terrific* racket
12. *nice* enough
13. a *terrific* day
14. *wonderful* things
15. absolutely *great* displays
16. that *wonderful* place

EXERCISE ONE

Rewrite the paragraph in the sample exercises, substituting more meaningful words for the dull ones.

Note: In the second paragraph, there is a deliberate mistake in grammar! Did you catch it? ". . . a police car came along, and he was nice. . . ." Was the police car nice? This is an example of the indefinite antecedent for the pronoun.

Idioms

There are certain expressions in our language that are regarded as correct for no particular grammatical reason. Indeed, sometimes these expressions do not really make much sense. When you say, "Don't go to pieces over it," you obviously don't mean that someone is going to fall apart. When you say that someone "has lost his head" about something, once again you do not mean that. These expressions are called *idiomatic*. Every language has such terms. Sometimes, instead of being complete expressions such as those just shown, *idioms* involve merely one or two words. In English you will find that many idiomatic expressions involve the use of prepositions after verbs. For example: His main interest centers (on, around) making a living.

The following is a list of commonly used idiomatic expressions:

1. One thing is *different from* another.
   I beg to *differ with* you.
2. You *take* something *from* someone - not *off of* him.
3. You *agree with* someone's idea, but you *agree to* do something.
4. They *compared* the Empire State Building *with* the World Trade Center. (This is as though they were setting them side by side.)
5. He proved himself *equal to* the task.
6. The lady announced that she was not *at home* to anyone.
7. He *preferred to* relax rather than to exert himself.
8. A baseball team *consists of* nine players. (Note: An alternative could be, A baseball team *comprises* nine players.)
9. He was *oblivious of* the tumult surrounding him.
10. It is necessary to *comply with* the law.
11. Gold is *superior to* tin in value.

The two following errors in style are among the most common in the language:

1. He chose the wrong business to go *into*.
2. She said that she would make all efforts *to definitely meet* him.

DICTION AND STYLE

Sentence 1 illustrates the rule that a sentence should not end with a preposition. In this case, it would be much more simple and effective to say

He chose the wrong business.

Sentence 2 demonstrates the stylistic error called a *split infinitive*. Notice that the verb *to meet* is split by the adverb *definitely*. The correct form should be:

She said that she definitely would make all efforts to meet him.

This rule is honored more in the books than in everyday language. Just as "It's me" had come to be accepted in common language, so has the occasional split infinitive.

Figures of Speech

Among the devices used to make language more colorful, lively, and precise are comparisons to which we give the name *figures of speech*. Among the most familiar are the following three:

1. *Simile*—a direct comparison making use of the words *like* and *as*.
2. *Metaphor*—an indirect or implied comparison in which two things are presented as being the same.
3. *Personification*—a device which gives a nonhuman object human attributes.

Illustrations:

He ran *like* a kid with the cops after him. (*simile*)
She *was an angel* of kindness. (*metaphor*)
The wind howled *angrily*. (*personification*)

Note: Any one of these figures of speech, *when it is overused*, becomes what is called a cliche—a tired simile or metaphor. You should try very hard to avoid such errors. No figure of speech at all is better, in terms of writing style, than one that is dull and common.

Another error that you may make in the use of figures of speech is to confuse or mix them. The name *mixed metaphor* is applied to such a mistake. For example:

The creature came at him *hissing like a lion*.

Since *hissing* is not normally an attribute of the lion, this comparison becomes laughable and confusing.

SEVEN

Logic and Organization

PRETEST

There is a statement made about each of the numbered sentences in the following groups. Blacken the letter of the number corresponding to the correct answer.

(1) Much criticism has been directed at the political structure of the United States. (2) Unfortunately, I can think of no other country with such political freedom. (3) Its basic strength is in the political liberty of its citizens. (4) For you to ignore this fact is to ignore political and social history.

1. Sentence 1 should be

   (1) placed after sentence 3
   (2) left where it is
   (3) omitted
   (4) placed after sentence 4
   (5) completed

2. In sentence 2, the word *Unfortunately* should be changed to

   (1) Wisely
   (2) Therefore
   (3) Actually
   (4) Because
   (5) Fortunately

3. Sentences 2 and 3 should be

   (1) reversed in order
   (2) left in the same order
   (3) combined into one sentence
   (4) omitted
   (5) joined by the word *while*

4. Sentence 4 should start with the words

   (1) To ignore
   (2) For me
   (3) For them
   (4) For us
   (5) This fact

---

(1) To learn that this was true of women stunned me. (2) I was shocked to see that woman are as capable of ego abuse as men. (3) Women, I believed, were real different. (4) I thought that in feminism I would find true cooperation.

5. Sentence 2 should be

   (1) the concluding sentence
   (2) joined to sentence 3 with the word *and*
   (3) after sentence 3
   (4) the first sentence
   (5) left as it is

6. In sentence 2, the word *women* should be

   (1) women
   (2) persons
   (3) people
   (4) the women
   (5) no change

7. In sentence 3 the word *real* should be

   (1) really
   (2) omitted
   (3) honest
   (4) especial
   (5) no change

8. Sentences 3 and 4 should be

   (1) combined, using the word *although*
   (2) combined, using the word *because*
   (3) left as they are
   (4) reversed in order
   (5) combined, using the word *but*

LOGIC AND ORGANIZATION

(1) The Western hero is a figure of loneliness and melancholy. (2) In other words, the image of the cowboy riding off into the sunset is typical of many Western films. (3) Such a hero is also shown as being shy of women. (4) However, he is rather withdrawn and quiet. (5) Even in today's world, the appeal of this type of character is still very strong. (6) Instead, the position of John Wayne as a folk hero is an e-ample of this power of identification. (7) It seems that for women as well as for men, the lure of the "strong, silent" type is still powerful. (8) It is a kind of "machismo" that is very hard to erase. (9) Actually, a close study of such modern films as *Star Wars* will reveal many elements of the successful Western. (10) The young man seeks revenge; the rugged adventurer hides a heart of gold beneath a rough surface; the old, wise man has secret powers; and, of course, the lovely, innocent lass—this time a princess—must be rescued. (11) Small wonder that this science-fiction film was so popular throughout the world.

9. Sentence 2 should begin with the words

   (1) For example
   (2) Because
   (3) While
   (4) However
   (5) no change

10. Sentence 2 should

    (1) be connected to Sentence 1 as it stands
    (2) be made into two sentences
    (3) begin the paragraph
    (4) be connected to Sentence 3 by the word *also*
    (5) no change

11. Sentence 4 should

    (1) begin with the words *He is rather*
    (2) begin with the word *Also*
    (3) begin with the word *Moreover*
    (4) begin with the word *Decidedly*
    (5) no change

WRITING

12. Sentence 6 should begin with the word(s)
    (1) The position of
    (2) The precision of
    (3) Obviously
    (4) Fortunately
    (5) no change

13. To divide these sentences into *three* paragraphs, you should begin the *second* and *third* paragraphs with the words
    (1) *The position of John Wayne* and *Actually, a close study*
    (2) *Such a hero* and *The young man*
    (3) *Even in today's world* and *Actually, a close study*
    (4) *Even in today's world* and *It seems that for women*
    (5) *However, he is* and *It is a kind of "machismo"*

14. Sentences 9 and 10 should be combined as follows:
    (1) the successful *Western, the young man*
    (2) the successful *Western. Having* the young man seeking
    (3) the successful *Western: The young man*
    (4) the successful *Western. By having* the young man seeking
    (5) the successful *Western.* Seeking revenge by the young man

15. In Sentence 11 the word *popular* should be
    (1) claimed
    (2) acclimated
    (3) excepted
    (4) rejoiced
    (5) no change

16. In sentence 8 the word *machismo* is in quotation marks because

    (1) it is a hard word
    (2) it is a regional expression
    (3) it is deliberately spelled wrong
    (4) it is slang
    (5) it is being emphasized

17. This paragraph should actually be divided into

    (1) two paragraphs
    (2) three paragraphs
    (3) four paragraphs
    (4) five paragraphs
    (5) no change

18. In sentence 9 the word *Actually* is an example of

    (1) a transition word
    (2) a word of emotion
    (3) a modifier
    (4) an introductory adjective
    (5) a misplaced modifier

19. The topic sentence of the first paragraph is

    (1) Sentence 1
    (2) Sentence 3
    (3) Sentence 4
    (4) Sentence 5
    (5) Sentence 8

PARAGRAPH DEVELOPMENT

1. The correctly written and clearly developed paragraph is the foundation stone of extended writing. At this point we reach a combining of forms and techniques—a discussion of the construction of understandable and clear paragraphs. Starting with a discussion of words and their meanings, we have progressed through a study of correct usage and correct, concise use of more advanced forms—notably the sentence. We have been proceeding in a step-by-step manner through a study of correct speech and writing.

Hold it, now! Don't jump off the train! Can you make head or tail of the preceding jumble of sentences? We certainly hope not! It is a disorganized grouping of sentences—full of words and punctuation—signifying nothing. But look:

2. We have been proceeding in a step-by-step manner through a study of correct speech and writing. Starting with a discussion of words and their meanings, we have progressed through a study of correct usage and correct use of more advanced forms—notably the sentence. At this point we must consider a combining of forms and techniques—a discussion of the construction of comprehensible, clear, and cogent *paragraphs*. For the correctly written and clearly developed *paragraph* is the foundation stone of extended writing.

In Number 2 we have a clearly written *paragraph* from which we can find a definition of what a paragraph is: a group of sentences **arranged in such a manner as to clarify or emphasize one idea or topic.** Frequently, that topic is **actually stated in the first sentence in the paragraph, which becomes known** as the *topic sentence.*

> Certainly no American can be surprised when told that sex plays an enormous role in selling. But how it works is frequently astonishing. Sex images have, of course, long been used by advertising writers, in print and on television. But the extent and depth of the "sex approach" are truly startling. A perfect example is illustrated in Dr. Dichter's famous study of the automobile. This is now known as "Mistress versus Wife."

Notice that in this case the first sentence states the topic: "Certainly no American can be surprised when told that sex plays an enormous role in selling." Obviously, then, the rest of the paragraph must be related to that idea. And it develops that idea—in the sense that it leads us toward further discussion of whatever general point the writer wishes to make. Notice also that the last sentence of the paragraph performs a double task: It summarizes the particular idea with which the paragraph has been dealing, and it shows the direction that the next paragraph will take. In this case, it is apparent that there is going to be a more detailed discussion of the "Mistress versus Wife" characteristics of sex in selling.

In handling the paragraph, then, the first requirement is that each sentence be connected to the overall idea of the paragraph, and that *each sentence stem from the preceding sentence* and flow into the succeeding one. There are different methods for developing that paragraph.

Development Through Details

In working out our paragraph, when we wish to support the topic sentence and make our point clearly, we make use of details and facts:

> The Kurds are the forgotten people of our time. Who are they? They are a mountain nation of almost 16 million people. Their land borders Iraq. While at one time they were allies of the United States, we have now forgotten them. Kurdish culture is being destroyed by the Iraqis. As a people they are being wiped out. However, not a voice is raised in protest.

Development Through Contrast

Sometimes, in order to emphasize a particular point, we compare or contrast one thing or idea with another:

> The quarterback and the center of a football team may be compared with the English and Spanish ships during the great battle which resulted in the defeat of the Spanish Armada. The center, huge, hulking, and made to hold his ground, is like the overwhelming Spanish galleons. They were powerful, heavily gunned, and heavily manned. And they were bulky and hard to handle. And so, generally, is the center. He is made to stay. The quarterback, however, is like the English ships. Lightly armed, made to sail swiftly and maneuver well, they ran rings around their opponents. And such is the quarterback—made for lightning runs and quick spins—to get where the enemy is not.

Development Through Point of View

This technique is used frequently in a paragraph designed to describe something. The writer must determine how he is looking at the scene he is describing—from his own viewpoint, from that of an outsider, or from within the scene itself:

> The room was high, dark, and gloomy in appearance. The long entrance hall plunged forward into what seemed a black cave. Glowing dimly in the darkness, a golden railing led upward along a stairway that curved into upper darkness. Along the wall that flanked the stairs, great dark hangings applied layers of black upon black. And just at the top of the broad steps a tiny bulb sent out flickers of golden light that were immediately swallowed by the enclosing darkness.

Development Through Sequence of Time

This technique is frequent in discussions of historical events, social movements, or simple accounts of personal experience:

> Even before the Indians appeared on American soil, it seems likely that great, primitive beasts roamed the land. They were followed centuries later by early humans who, according to some authorities, came across the Bering Straits from Europe. As the ages moved on, the human creatures adapted themselves to climate and conditions, while the ancient beasts died out. Then, as time went on, in America as elsewhere, the primitive human evolved into the kind of creature we now call man.

Development Through Classification

This device can be most useful in discussing varieties of uses of particular objects or theories. It lends itself to great exactness and clearness of thought:

> The uses of the automobile may be placed into three broad categories: general usefulness, comfort, and pleasure. To answer the demand for the great variety of uses to which cars are put, manufacturers have produced the station wagon, the small van, the "jeep," and the small truck. For comfort there are the large roomy sedans, the well-padded two-door elite cars, and the small but equally well-padded runabouts. And for the sport-car enthusiast there is a whole variety of stick-shift, bucket seat, snappy small cars, with powerful engines, low profiles, and excessive speed potential.

In any piece of extended writing, of course, it is usually desirable, if not actually necessary, to use a variety of paragraph designs. The greater the variety, the greater the interest in the reading. Usually one can express oneself better and more colorfully by avoiding a sameness of tone and atmosphere in writing.

The plan for the development of a proper paragraph is something like a road map: each new sentence should lead easily and clearly into the next one. Each idea should provide a sensible link with the following idea. From the first sentence to the last, there should be a smooth, easy-to-follow route. Well-written, meaningful sentences—like accurate directions—enable you to get rid of vagueness and inaccuracy in your writing of paragraphs.

Read the following with extreme care:

(1) There was a man named Jabez Stone, lived at Cross Corners, New Hampshire. (2) If he planted corn, he got borers; if he planted potatoes,

he got blight. (3) He wasn't a bad man to start with, but he was an unlucky man. (4) He had good enough land, but it didn't prosper him; he had a decent wife and children, but the more children he had, the less there was to feed them. (5) There's some folks bound to be like that, apparently. (6) If stones cropped up in his neighbor's field, boulders boiled up in his; if he had a horse with the spavins, he'd trade it for one with the staggers and give something extra. (7) But one day Jabez Stone got sick of the whole business.

A road map of this paragraph will create a puzzle indeed. Sentence 1 introduces a character and gives his background. Sentence 2 sounds like a step in the right direction. But sentence 3 sends us racing around on a detour. The "bad man to start with" has no relation to what has gone before; it almost seems a case of the cart before the horse. Sentence 4 sends us back on our tracks rather than taking us forward toward our destination. Sentences 5 and 6 again seem out of place and out of correct order. The net result is that the final statement, instead of being a sharp, strong statement of the purpose of the paragraph, seems to have no special point at all.

EXERCISE ONE

Rewrite the paragraph about Jabez Stone in what you feel is the most effective fashion. Before you begin, think carefully of where you want to go.

Now here is the paragraph as it appears in Stephen Vincent Benet's great short story *The Devil and Daniel Webster*.

(1) There was a man named Jabez Stone, lived at Cross Corners, New Hampshire. (2) He wasn't a bad man to start with, but he was an unlucky man. (3) If he planted corn, he got borers; if he planted potatoes, he got blight. (4) He had good enough land, but it didn't prosper him; he had a decent wife and children, but the more children he had, the less there was to feed them. (5) If stones cropped up in his neighbor's field, boulders boiled up in his; if he had a horse with the spavins, he'd trade it for one with the staggers and give something extra. (6) There's some folks bound to be like that apparently. (7) But one day Jabez Stone got sick of the whole business.

Notice the trip Benet has taken you on: You start with Jabez Stone at Cross Corners and proceed to his "getting sick of the whole business." Looking back you can see the highway you have traveled: the bad luck—and illustrations of it; his responsibilities and his inability, *through no fault* of his own, to carry them; and a comparison with his neighbors, to Jabez' disadvantage.

Examine carefully sentence 6. If that were the final sentence, the whole story would stop right there. Certainly the paragraph would. But remember that the last sentence of a good paragraph *must do two things*: (1) complete the thought of the paragraph itself, and (2) reach forward to lead directly into the following paragraph.

Examine sentence 7: "But one day Jabez Stone got sick of the whole business." Obviously something more is going to happen; you are given a clue that a change will take place—and are lured forward by the Pied Piper storyteller.

Up to now we have been looking at the overall nature of the paragraph—its general construction and direction. We saw how necessary it is for each sentence to follow clearly from the preceding one—how important it is for each sentence to lead meaningfully into the next.

Now let us try to look for something different. Let us, as though using X rays, probe beneath the skin of the paragraph and watch the functioning of the muscle and the tissue.

Notice, first, the use of the word *but* in sentences 2 and 4.

He wasn't a bad man to start with, *but* he was an unlucky man.

The conjunction *but*—a word of transition—acts like a broken field runner in a football game; he is always going forward, but he switches and swivels back and forth to guarantee his forward drive.

Look at the two *buts* in sentence 4:

He had good enough land, *but* it didn't prosper him; he had a decent wife and children, *but* the more children he had . . .

Now study the last sentence:

But one day Jabez Stone got sick of the whole business.

Here the word *but* starts the sentence. You can see, by looking back at sentence 2, that this has been the goal of the entire paragraph. Jabez Stone reacts to his bad luck, and he is going to do something about it. This last sentence, then, sums up one paragraph and leads directly and strongly into the next. It is an excellent concluding sentence.

TRANSITIONAL WORDS

You will notice that the word *but* is referred to as a *transitional word*. Its function is to carry along the meaning of the sentence—to connect one part with another. *But* there is an additional function that such a word performs. It indicates a change of direction in the thought and meaning. Notice that the *but* in the previous sentence signals an added meaning that is to be presented.

Actually, there are many transition words which give many different signals. As the following list and examples will indicate, transitional words are important in clarifying meaning and understanding.

Transitional words that indicate the relationship of:

1. *Additional ideas:* in addition, also, furthermore, besides, again, moreover.
2. *Comparison:* likewise, similarly, in the same way, and, in the same manner.
3. *Contrast:* on the other hand, but, however, nevertheless, at the same time, yet.
4. *Example:* for example, to illustrate, for instance, that is, such as.
5. *Result:* as a consequence, consequently, thus, as a result, it follows that, therefore, as we can see, from this.
6. *Space:* above, below, beside, next to, to the right (left), beyond, behind.
7. *Summing up:* in conclusion, on the whole, finally.
8. *Time:* first, now, meanwhile, eventually, later, then.

Transitional words may be used within paragraphs as well as to link two paragraphs together. In addition to making things clearer, transitional words provide for smoother expression and more pleasant reading. Of course, if they are misused, they cause confusion and lack of understanding.

EXERCISE ONE

In each of the following paragraphs; there are four underlined transition words. Blacken the space which corresponds to the incorrectly used word. If there are no errors, blacken space 5.

1. The bats fly from the caves at Carlsbad with the approach of night. <u>At first</u>, one or two make their appearance. Above the
   ₁
   heads of the people they circle. <u>Soon</u> a mighty swarm comes
   ₂
   out. Circling ever higher, they <u>eventually</u> form a huge cloud.
   ₃
   <u>Then</u> they disappear over the countryside.
   ₄

   1.   1 2 3 4 5

2. <u>As might be expected</u>, the melting snows caused flooding in
   ₁
   the valley areas. <u>Notwithstanding</u> the already overflowing
   ₂
   rivers, the danger to nearby towns increased greatly. <u>Consequently</u>, it was thought advisable to remove all the people
   ₃
   from their homes. <u>As a result</u>, there was little loss of life.
   ₄

   2.   1 2 3 4 5

3. The similarity of newly born puppies to newly born kittens is remarkable. Kittens are tiny, squirmy things; <u>similarly</u>,
   ₁
   little puppies appear minute and in constant motion. <u>In addition</u>, neither opens its eyes until some time has gone by.
   ₂
   <u>However</u>, each is totally in need of its mother. And each, <u>in
   ₃
   the same way</u>, finds it impossible to move steadily on its feet.
   ₄

   3.   1 2 3 4 5

LOGIC AND ORGANIZATION

141

EXERCISE TWO

Making use of the accompanying transition words, link the following sentences into coherent, logical paragraphs. Write these transition words in the blanks across from the sentences in which you feel they should appear.

meanwhile, despite this, for example, however, consequently, for instance, on the other hand, but, finally, as a result, in conclusion, eventually, in addition to, therefore, but, such as, on the whole, because

1. (1) John's brother was considerably older than John.   1. _____
   (2) John was a much better dancer. _____
   (3) There was a considerable amount of envy between them. _____
   (4) They were still very fond of each other. _____

2. (1) The need for control of bad air was established years ago.   2. _____
   (2) Means for handling the problem were discussed seriously. _____
   (3) Additional sources of bad air were developed. _____
   (4) The government itself stepped into the matter. _____

3. (1) The problem of peace in the Mideast concerns the world.   3. _____
   (2) There are some who constantly seem to be playing with fire. _____
   (3) Many of the steps toward peace are made difficult. _____
   (4) It is hoped that cool heads and minds will remain on top. _____

4. (1) An understanding of words stems from constant reading.   4. _____
   (2) It is important to concentrate on teaching reading at all levels. _____
   (3) Introducing simplified reading texts at an early age will help. _____
   (4) It is not a problem for the schools alone. _____

5. (1) Growing older makes one sensitive to weather changes. 5. _____

(2) What was once regarded as "brisk" weather becomes "freezing." _____

(3) Many people seek to move to warmer sections of the country. _____

(4) The sun belt has become a booming area of population growth. _____

ORGANIZATION

(1) In our discussion of the paragraph we have spoken of the need to maintain a sense of direction and purpose in our writing. (2) We have studied very clearly at least one paragraph from the pen of an outstanding author. (3) In our study we have observed how carefully a writer goes about choosing good, exact words to develop his meaning. (4) Certainly, we have arrived at the conclusion that to write clearly is not always easy.

If, however, you can school yourself to construct solid, meaningful paragraphs, you can reach the point where you can claim clearness of expression, if not beauty. And, truthfully speaking, there can be beauty even in simple, direct, exact expression. At this point, make such expression your goal.

A paragraph is simply an organization of sentences around a theme. The purpose of the paragraph is fourfold:

1. To present and develop a new idea.
2. To show how this new idea stems from the previous material.
3. To advance thought clearly to the following idea and paragraph.
4. To control the flow of thought, admitting only necessary material and leaving out extra material.

If the paragraph revolves around a single theme or idea, it is important that this theme be identified at the outset. And it is. Every paragraph has a *topic sentence*. This sentence—usually the first or second of the paragraph—is like a school banner or a town sign. It tells the reader what the paragraph is all about. It identifies the place in the road. It looks back as though to say, "This is where we've come from," and turns ahead to say, "That is where we're going." And the paragraph which grows out of the topic sentence fills in between the "where from?" and the "where to?"

LOGIC AND ORGANIZATION

The first paragraph is different from other paragraphs only in the sense that it is charged with an important task: It must be so interesting, exciting, and important that the reader wants to continue reading. The first paragraph, therefore, must ask striking questions or present striking ideas. It must hook the reader.

Examine closely the first paragraph of this section. Notice that although it is an opening paragraph, it appears to continue the course of what has been discussed before. In addition, this paragraph establishes the direction of the chapter which follows:

> The topic sentence sets the tone: "We have spoken of the need to maintain a sense of direction and purpose." Sentence 2 adds some detailed support of the first statement, and it serves to refresh our memory. Sentence 3 sharpens our focus a bit more and reminds us of our study of "good, exact words." Sentence 4 sums up the brief opening paragraph and indicates that more discussion in a slightly different key is to follow. The last sentence leads into the opening sentence of the next paragraph, as though it were a runner handing his baton to his relay partner.

Note: In studying the opening paragraph of the section, you will find that any attempt to rewrite it with the sentences in a different order will result in the destruction of the clearness and meaning of the paragraph. This will illustrate one of the techniques of paragraph development—through *a listing of facts or specific examples*.

EIGHT

Vocabulary

Every Election Day, whether on a national or local level, most politicians claim to fear voter *apathy*. Suppose that you really have no idea what the word means: Is it too much voter turnout? too little? the wrong kind? What clues are there to help you figure out the meaning? Look at the word:

a path y

Suppose you recognize that *path* appears in the words *path*etic, *path*os, and sym*path*y, and remember that *path* has something to do with feeling and emotion. Good!

Take the *a* part of the word. Think of words like *a*typical, *a*theist, and *a*moral, and gather that *a* must have something to do with *no* or *not* or *not any*.

Now you can piece together some kind of meaning: no feeling.

The *y* is a syllable that makes a word a noun; it indicates the state or quality of something.

Put the jigsaw together, and you get "no feeling about," which is just what *apathy* means: lack of concern; indifference.

There are three parts of a word which, when you know them, can help you to figure out the meaning of most words. They are called the stem (root), the prefix, and the suffix. The *stem* is the core of the word, because it gives the basic meaning; the *prefix* shows the direction of the word—toward, away from, with, against, etc.; the *suffix* indicates the part of speech of the word—adjective, noun, adverb.

Let us go back to the stem *path*—feeling. If you have the word *sym-path-y*, and you know that the prefix *sym* means *with*, then you know the word *sympathy* means a feeling *with* or *toward* somebody. If you have the same stem—*path*—but the prefix *anti*, forming *antipathy*, you may figure out that *anti* means against. Therefore, *antipathy* means a feeling against, or a strong dislike.

WRITING

What follows is a list of some of the most common stems, prefixes, and suffixes. If you become familiar with them, you should be able to determine the meanings of most words you read.

Note: The stem usually appears at the heart of the word, though it does not have a fixed place; the prefix is always at the beginning of the word; the suffix is always the tail.

Stem	Meaning	Illustration
ag	act, urge, force	agitate
alt	high	altitude
aud	hear, hearing	audible
cad (cas, cid)	fall	accident
cant	sing	cantata
cap (capt, ceipt, cept)	take, seize, hold	accept
carn (charn)	flesh	carnal
ced (cess, ceed)	go, yield	proceed
corpos (corpor, corps)	body	incorporate
cred	believe	incredible
cur (curat)	care, care for	security
curr (cours, curs)	run	recurrent
dict	speak	predict
dign	worthy	indignity
duct	to lead, bring	conductor
fac (fact, fic)	make, do	manufacture
fer	to bear, carry	transfer
frang (fract, frag)	break	fracture
fus	melt, pour	fusion
ger (gerat, gest)	carry on, bear	gestation
grad (gress)	step, go	progress
graph (gram)	write	autograph
juc (ject)	throw, hurl	projectile
junct (jug)	join	junction
lect	gather, choose	collect
leg	send	delegate
loc	place	location
log	word, science, study	astrology
loq (locut)	speak, talk	elocution
mir (mirat)	wonder	miracle
mis (miss, mit)	send	transmit
ped	foot	pedestrian
pend (pens)	hang, weigh, pay	pendant
pon (pos, posit)	place	deposit
spec (spect)	look	spectacle
tang (tact, tain)	touch	tangible

VOCABULARY

terre	earth, ground	subterranean
therm	heat	thermometer
vert	turn	introvert
vid (vis)	see	invisible
voc (vocat)	call	vocation

The *prefix* of a word gives, in effect, its direction. You have seen, in the preceding list, that the stem *ject* means *to throw* or *to hurl*. With various prefixes, you can "hurl" in different directions:

*re*ject—to throw *back*
*in*ject—to throw *into*
*pro*ject—to throw *forth*
*de*ject—to throw *down*
*inter*ject—to throw *between*

Here is a list of common prefixes:

Prefix	Meaning	Illustration
a	not, without	apathy
ab, a, abs	separation, away from	absent
ad, ac, at	to, toward	attraction
ante	before, in front	anteroom
anti	against	antipathy
bene	well, good	benefit
cata	down	catastrophe
de	down, away from	descend
dia	through	diameter
dis	opposite of, apart	dislike
epi	upon, for	epidermis
ex, e	out of, from	exit
hyper	excess, too much	hypertension
hypo	into, under, insufficient	hypodermic
in *(in verbs)*	into, toward	incline
in *(in adjectives, adverbs, and nouns)*	not	inaudible
ob, op, oc	opposition, against	opponent
pen	almost	peninsula
per	through (time, space)	permit
pre	before	precede
sub	under	submarine
syn, syl, sym	with, together	symphony
trans	beyond, across	transmit
ultra	beyond, extreme	ultraviolet
re	back	regress

WRITING

The *suffix* is the final part of a word. It determines basically what part of speech the word will be. Here are some common suffixes:

Suffix	Meaning	Part of Speech	Illustration
able	capable of, able	usually adjective	understandable
acy	state of being, state	noun	lunacy
al	act of, relating to	adjective	casual
an	one who	noun	physician
ant, ent	one who	noun	superintendent
ar	relating to; one who	adjective; noun	peculiar
ee	one to whom	noun	payee
er, or	one who	noun	manager
ful	full	adjective	beautiful
ian	one who is killed	noun	optician
ion, tion, sion	state of being	noun	tension
ive	able to	adjective	responsive
less	without, lacking	adjective	helpless
ly	in such a manner	adverb	casually
ment	that which does	noun	impediment
ous	full of, characterized by	adjective	gorgeous
tude	quality of	noun	mangitude
ence	a lack of ability	noun	sufficience
y	characterized by, inclined to	adjective	grouchy

The addition of prefixes and suffixes affect the spelling of words. Look at the word *satisfied*; add the prefix *dis*. Is one *s* replaced by the other? Are there two *s*'s? The answer is if the word itself begins with an *s*, the addition of a prefix that ends with an *s* gives a doubled letter:

    dis-satisfied—dissatisfied

If the word begins with a letter other than *s*, there will not be a doubled letter:

    disappoint—disappoint

The same rule holds true for other prefixes:

    mis-spell—misspell
    un-necessary—unnecessary
    im-material—immaterial

The suffix *ly* is frequently added to words without otherwise changing them: love-ly; immediate-ly; immediate-ly; definite-ly; attractive-ly.

The one important exception is the word *true*. Here you drop the final *e* to make *truly*.

VOCABULARY

EXERCISE ONE

Try to figure out the meaning and part of speech of each of the following words. Write your answers on the blanks at the right.

1. incompetence   _____
2. incessantly   _____
3. regressive   _____
4. diathermy   _____
5. subterranean   _____
6. synthetic   _____
7. phonogram   _____
8. revert   _____
9. incredulous   _____
10. projectile   _____

OTHER STEMS AND PREFIXES

Stem	Meaning	Illustration
bellum	war	bellicose, antebellum
chromo	color	polychrome
chrono	time	chronology
civis	citizen	civil
fide, fidel	loyal, faithful	fidelity
mob, mov, mot	move	mobility
phon, phono	sound	phonograph
port	carry, bear	portable
scrib, script	write	prescribe
tele	distant	television
volv	turn	revolver

Prefix	Meaning	Illustration
ambi	both	ambivalent
auto	self	automatic
bi	two	bicycle
circum	around	circumnavigate
extra	beyond, above	extraordinary
intra	within	intravenous
mono	single	monoplane
pan	all	**Pan-American**
poly	many	polytheism
semi, hemi	half	hemisphere
super	above, over	supersonic
un	not	unknown

EXERCISE TWO

Break down each of the following words into separate syllable meanings. Write your answers in the space provided.

1. antipathetic
2. polygon
3. conversion
4. infidelity
5. benediction
6. intermittent
7. extrasensory
8. unsympathetic
9. invocation
10. bipartisan
11. autonomous
12. amorality
13. transitional
14. intractable
15. interjection

1. _____
2. _____
3. _____
4. _____
5. _____
6. _____
7. _____
8. _____
9. _____
10. _____
11. _____
12. _____
13. _____
14. _____
15. _____

NINE

Posttest

SPELLING, PUNCTUATION, AND CAPITALIZATION

In each of the following groups of words, one may be misspelled.
In the answer column, blacken the space that corresponds to the number of the misspelled word. If no word is misspelled, blacken space 5.

1. (1) feind   (3) friend   1. 1 2 3 4 5
   (2) tireless   (4) conscience

2. (1) doesn't   (3) critic   2. 1 2 3 4 5
   (2) agreeable   (4) column

3. (1) intelligent (3) advise   3. 1 2 3 4 5
   (2) supervice   (won't)

4. (1) missionery (3) entrance   4. 1 2 3 4 5
   (2) entirely   (4) conceive

5. (1) argument   (3) recede   5. 1 2 3 4 5
   (2) evidentally (4) control

6. (1) scheduled   (3) lively   6. 1 2 3 4 5
   (2) proceedure (4) Wednesday

7. (1) inconvienient (3) lighten   7. 1 2 3 4 5
   (2) likely   (4) fifth

8. (1) site   (3) existence   8. 1 2 3 4 5
   (2) interrupt   (4) hygeine

152 WRITING

9. (1) prescribe   (3) useful   9. 1 2 3 4 5
    (2) mileage   (4) tonage

10. (1) preparation   (3) careful   10. 1 2 3 4 5
    (2) unvieling   (4) apologize

In each of the following passages, there may be an error in punctuation or capitalization. Blacken the space in the answer column that corresponds to the number of the error. If there is no error, blacken space 5.

11. <u>his</u> favorite subjects were <u>science</u>, <u>Spanish</u>, and <u>American</u> history.
    1   2   3   4
11. 1 2 3 4 5

12. <u>His</u> friends deserted him<u>;</u> his girlfriend scorned him<u>:</u> his favorite <u>dog</u> bit him.
   1   2 3   4
12. 1 2 3 4 5

13. <u>Did</u> he<u>,</u> when he received the great news<u>,</u> burst into pleased <u>laughter.</u>
   1   2   3   4
13. 1 2 3 4 5

14. "<u>I</u> claim, as <u>Mayor</u> of this town, that <u>City</u> <u>Hall</u> belongs to me."
    1   2   3   4
14. 1 2 3 4 5

15. "Halt!<u>"</u> the sentry shouted<u>.</u> <u>"</u>Halt! I'll shoot!<u>"</u>
         1   2   3   4
15. 1 2 3 4 5

16. For some strange reason, Alice<u>,</u> even as an adult<u>,</u> called her father <u>mr.</u> <u>Franklin</u>.
                               1   2   3 4
16. 1 2 3 4 5

17. She asked <u>Brother</u> <u>Francis</u> if she might visit her <u>brother</u> in the <u>monastery</u>.
            1   2   3   4
17. 1 2 3 4 5

18. The women were at various moments infuriated<u>,</u> humiliated<u>,</u> insulted, and hurt by his <u>remarks</u>.
                                                      1   2   3   4
18. 1 2 3 4 5

POSTTEST

19. $\underset{1}{\underline{T}}$homas was interested in study and meditation; and his $\underset{2}{\underline{\text{stu}d\text{y}}}$ $\underset{3}{\underline{\text{and}}}$ $\underset{4}{\underline{b}}$rother approved of these interests.

   19. 1 2 3 4 5

20. $\underset{1}{\underline{O}}$n visiting the capita$\underset{2}{\underline{l,}}$ they were particularly thrille$\underset{3}{\underline{d}}$ by the sight of the $\underset{4}{\underline{C}}$apitol.

   20. 1 2 3 4 5

GRAMMAR AND USAGE

In each of the following passages, there may be an error in grammar or usage. Blacken the space in the answer column that corresponds to the number of the error. If there is no error, blacken space 5.

1. He $\underset{1}{\underline{\text{asked}}}$ David $\underset{2}{\underline{\text{politely}}}$ where the game $\underset{3}{\underline{\text{was}}}$ $\underset{4}{\underline{\text{at}}}$.

   1. 1 2 3 4 5

2. $\underset{1}{\underline{\text{The}}}$ championship team $\underset{2}{\underline{\text{consisted}}}$ of Frank, Larry, Dave, Henry, $\underset{3}{\underline{\text{and}}}$ $\underset{4}{\underline{\text{I}}}$.

   2. 1 2 3 4 5

3. It's quite clear $\underset{1}{\underline{\text{that}}}$ $\underset{2}{\phantom{\text{that}}}$ the judges do not consider $\underset{3}{\underline{\text{your's}}}$ to be the $\underset{4}{\underline{\text{best}}}$ answer.

   3. 1 2 3 4 5

4. $\underset{1}{\underline{\text{Maria and Kathy}}}$ waited $\underset{2}{\underline{\text{breathlessly}}}$ for the announcement, $\underset{3}{\underline{\text{both}}}$ girls hoping she had won the high awar$\underset{4}{\underline{d}}$.

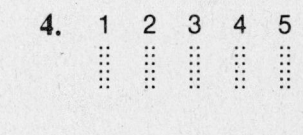

   4. 1 2 3 4 5

5. They felt that $\underset{1}{\underline{\text{despite}}}$ all their efforts they $\underset{2}{\underline{\text{had}}}$ $\underset{3}{\underline{\text{made}}}$ $\underset{4}{\underline{\text{no real}}}$ progress toward a just peace.

   5. 1 2 3 4 5

6. $\underset{1}{\underline{\text{After hearing}}}$ our side $\underset{2}{\underline{\text{of the story}}}$ the teacher insisted $\underset{3}{\underline{\text{that}}}$ my brother and $\underset{4}{\underline{\text{me}}}$ had to make up the homework.

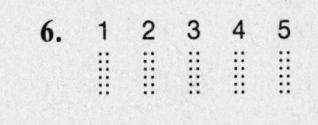

   6. 1 2 3 4 5

7. She $\underset{1}{\underline{\text{moved}}}$ slowly and $\underset{2}{\underline{\text{real}}}$ $\underset{3}{\underline{\text{carefully}}}$ through what $\underset{4}{\underline{\text{appeared}}}$ to $\underline{\text{be}}$ a swamp.

   7. 1 2 3 4 5

8. He felt that he <u>had become</u> what he <u>was</u> because, over the
                    1   2

   course of years, that <u>was</u> the way his mother <u>raised</u> him.
                      3   4

9. Because she <u>learned</u> to drive so <u>quickly</u>, <u>they</u> felt that <u>they</u>
   should grant her a license immediately.

10. It's very obvious that his parents <u>disapprove</u> of <u>him</u> learn-
    ing <u>to fly</u> at such an early age.

11. When he <u>saw</u> how they <u>had reacted</u> to his accusations, he
    felt <u>surprisingly</u> <u>unhappily</u>.

12. He <u>indicated</u> that <u>he</u> <u>didn't</u> particularly care to <u>who</u> I gave
    the reward.

13. <u>They</u> told me <u>they</u> planned <u>to go</u> before <u>Wednesday</u>.

14. I <u>admire</u> the fact <u>that</u> he stuck so <u>courageously</u> to his
    <u>principals</u>.

15. The club members <u>told</u> Harry that <u>they</u> appreciated <u>his</u>
    dancing and singing for <u>their</u> organization.

16. Do you <u>honestly</u> think that <u>either the boy</u> or his sisters <u>are</u>
    to blame?

17. For <u>all of us to succeed</u> in this undertaking, everybody <u>must</u>
    do <u>their</u> level best.

18. It <u>is</u> economically <u>necessary</u> to make sure that <u>this</u> entire
    shipment of new cars <u>get</u> to the port on time.

POSTTEST

19. Her attitude, while driving across the desert, was not clear
          1   2
    to her friends and to me.
       3   4

20. She informed her friend that her stubbornness presented
          1   2   3
    a great problem to their friendship.
                        4

21. Just before the big race, the crowd asked the tipster whom
        1   2   3
    he thought was going to win.
              4

22. Carolyn was really certain that her mother would not
                1   2   3
    permit Bill and she, to go to the movie without a chaperone.
                  4

23. He is as good if not better than his brother as a ballplayer.
          1   2   3   4

24. When your sure of your facts, you can be more confident
         1   2   3
    of your ability to argue.
       4

DICTION AND STYLE

In each of the following sentences, one section is in italics. If any of the alternatives listed below corrects or improves that section, blacken the space of the appropriate number. If no change is necessary, blacken space 5.

1. The boys went into their shack in order to *exchange views on their problems.*
   (1) air their opinions
   (2) vent their opinions
   (3) rap about their problems
   (4) interrelate about their problems
   (5) no change

2. The policeman said the suspect had *transgressed* the law as she saw it.
   (1) averted
   (2) evaded
   (3) broken
   (4) obstructed
   (5) no change

3. To perpetrate such a plan, he felt, would be *just plain mean*.
   (1) just plain nasty
   (2) just plainly mean
   (3) dreadfully unkind
   (4) just plain awful
   (5) no change

4. Her soothing voice was *like oil on troubled waters*. The italicized section is an example of
   (1) a simile
   (2) a personification
   (3) a metaphor
   (4) contrast
   (5) cause and effect

5. Regardless of his position at this time, *being that* he once broke the law, he must be punished.
   (1) being
   (2) seeing that
   (3) since
   (4) omit
   (5) no change

6. As far as I am concerned, it will be *alright* for them to take their leave.
   (1) OK
   (2) satisfactorily
   (3) all right
   (4) allright
   (5) no change

POSTTEST

7. Despite the doctor's warning, he continued to *itch* his wound.
   (1) scratch
   (2) itch at
   (3) stitch
   (4) avoid
   (5) no change

8. She drove carefully, but the accident *couldn't hardly* be avoided.
   (1) didn't hardly
   (2) wasn't hardly avoidable
   (3) could hardly be
   (4) couldn't hardly have been
   (5) no change

9. They decided to shift their headquarters, *irregardless* of the bad results.
   (1) disregarding
   (2) regarding
   (3) disregardless
   (4) regardless
   (5) no change

10. Responding to their appeal, Howard found them *all ready* to escape.
    (1) already
    (2) allready
    (3) already
    (4) all-ready
    (5) no change

11. It was spring; the sun *smiled* down upon the countryside. *Smiled* is an example of
    (1) a metaphor
    (2) a simile
    (3) personification
    (4) a description
    (5) a mixed metaphor

12. "This little fellow," he said, "is cute, smart, and *perspicacious*
   (1) comprehensive
   (2) loquacious
   (3) sharp
   (4) intellectual
   (5) no change

SENTENCE STRUCTURE

In each of the following statements, an italicized section may contain an error in sentence structure. In the answer column, blacken the space of the alternative choice which corrects or improves the underlined section. If no change is necessary, blacken space 5.

1. *Listening to his singing the song was obviously a hit.*
   (1) The song, listening to his singing, was obviously a hit.
   (2) While listening to his singing, obviously the song was a hit.
   (3) While listening to his singing, it was obvious that the song was a hit.
   (4) Listening to his singing, they could tell that the song was a hit.
   (5) no change

2. They worried about her mental condition, *having lost all her money.*
   (1) since having lost all her money
   (2) since she lost all her money
   (3) being she lost all her money
   (4) losing all her money
   (5) no change

POSTTEST

3. *We were frightened by the noises. We fled immediately.*
   (1) Being we were frightened by the noises, we fled immediately.
   (2) Being that we were frightened by the noises, we fled immediately.
   (3) Because we were frightened by the noises, we fled immediately.
   (4) The noises frightened us, we fled immediately.
   (5) no change

4. *Challenged by the sentry, it was a shock to him.*
   (1) Challenged by the sentry, it came as a shock to him.
   (2) Being challenged by the sentry, it was a shock to him.
   (3) Being that he was challenged by the sentry, he was shocked.
   (4) Being challenged by the sentry shocked him.
   (5) no change

5. *The train rolled into the station pulled by a diesel engine.*
   (1) The train rolled into the station which was pulled by a diesel engine.
   (2) The train, pulled by a diesel engine, rolled into the station.
   (3) The train rolled into the station by a diesel engine.
   (4) Pulled by a diesel engine into the station rolled the train.
   (5) no change

6. *She awakened early in the morning, and then she showered, and then she left.*
   (1) She awakened early in the morning, showered, and then left.
   (2) She awakened early in the morning. And then she showered, and then she left.
   (3) She awakened early in the morning. Then she showered and left.
   (4) She awakened early in the morning after showering, and then she left.
   (5) no change

7. His shyness made it impossible for him to step forward to *except* the prize.
   (1) expect
   (2) accept
   (3) accepting
   (4) expecting
   (5) no change

8. The guidance counselor *advised* her about her program for the next semester.
   (1) adviced
   (2) counciled
   (3) revised
   (4) admonished
   (5) no change

9. Many women feel that men have been overbearing, demanding, and *they humiliate their wives*.
   (1) and, in addition, they humiliate their wives
   (2) humiliating toward there wives
   (3) humiliating toward their wives
   (4) humility toward their wives
   (5) no change

10. It is discouraging to read about so much crime, *poverty, and terror. And war too.*
    (1) poverty, and terror. And war also.
    (2) poverty, and terror. And also warfare.
    (3) poverty, and terror. And there is also war.
    (4) poverty, terror, and war.
    (5) no change

11. My mother was delighted to learn of *me doing* so well at the piano.
    (1) I doing so well
    (2) my doing so well
    (3) my well doing
    (4) my doing so good
    (5) no change

POSTTEST

LOGIC AND ORGANIZATION

Read each of the following passages and the questions that relate to them. Pick the best answer to each question and blacken the corresponding space on the answer grids at the right.

(1) The spoken and written tongues of all peoples seem to have certain sayings or slogans which reflect the attitudes of the various cultures toward life, work, God, and the world in general. **(2)** Our language, too, is filled with such sayings. **(3)** Sometimes they seem to support one another; indeed, they sometimes offer contrasting points of view. **(4)** For example: "The devil makes work for idle hands" apparently contradicts the well-known "All work and no play makes Jack a dull boy." **(5)** The need to be ambitious and independent is illustrated by two popular sayings: "Opportunity knocks but once" and "Heaven helps him who helps himself." **(6)** Another plea to do one's best and to compete as well as possible comes in the form of: "The devil takes the hindmost." **(7)** One curious fact emerges from a study of the folk sayings of various nations and peoples. **(8)** Despite many differences in climate, geography, society, and history, there seem to be more similarities than differences in outlook toward the large, universal problems. **(9)** And you can easily see why this is true.

1. Sentence 1 is an example of a
   (1) topic sentence
   (2) leading statement
   (3) conclusion
   (4) transitional sentence
   (5) summarizing statement

2. In sentence 2 the word *too* should be
   (1) however
   (2) therefore
   (3) consequently
   (4) though
   (5) no change

3. Sentence 3 should be written
   (1) as two sentences with the second one beginning with *Indeed*
   (2) as a compound sentence with the second clause introduced by *and indeed*.
   (3) as a compound sentence with the second clause beginning *sometimes they*
   (4) as a compound sentence with the second clause beginning *obviously*
   (5) no change

4. In Sentence 4 the expression *For example* introduces
   (1) a contrast
   (2) a reason
   (3) an illustration
   (4) a time sequence
   (5) cause and effect

5. If this were to be broken into three paragraphs, the second and third paragraphs should start with
   (1) sentences 3 and 6
   (2) sentences 3 and 7
   (3) sentences 4 and 7
   (4) sentences 5 and 7
   (5) no change

6. The overall impression of the paragraph is that
   (1) all peoples are different
   (2) all languages seem the same
   (3) differences in geography, society, and climate prevent understanding among peoples
   (4) most peoples regard the large, universal problems in much the same way
   (5) there are really no differences among peoples

7. Sentence 9 should be
   (1) just before sentence 8
   (2) at the very beginning
   (3) after sentence 4
   (4) omitted
   (5) unchanged

POSTTEST

(1) The threat of the great new supertankers is not confined to the environment alone. (2) All the world knows of the dangers of pollution of land and sea as a result of tanker leaks and crack-ups. (3) Also less attention is paid to the menace of these monsters in the sea lanes. (4) An example is the *Torrey Canyon*. (5) These great vessels are completely helpless if anything happens to their automatic steering devices. (6) There is no chance to change to manual controls. (7) Secondly, it takes an enormous amount of time to stop one of the huge ships at sea. (8) Thirdly, there have been many accidents at sea because of this defect. (9) On the other hand it seems that means should be developed to overcome these handicaps.

8. Sentence 1 indicates that
   (1) there has been some previous discussion of the subject
   (2) this is the introduction of a new topic for discussion
   (3) this paragraph is going to contradict what has been said before
   (4) this paragraph will discuss another aspect of a previously mentioned matter
   (5) the author seems in favor of new and larger tankers

9. In sentence 3 the word *Also* should be
   (1) In addition
   (2) Nevertheless
   (3) As a result
   (4) However
   (5) no change

10. Sentence 4 should be
    (1) omitted
    (2) added to sentence 3 with the word *and*
    (3) placed after sentence 2
    (4) used as a concluding statement
    (5) no change

11. In sentence 8 the word *Thirdly* should be
    (1) omitted
    (2) Also
    (3) Despite this
    (4) They say
    (5) no change

12. In sentence 9 the phrase *On the other hand* should be
    (1) Obviously
    (2) Notwithstanding
    (3) omitted
    (4) As a result
    (5) no change

TEN

Answers and Analysis

PRETEST

1.	**(1)**	attend<u>a</u>nce	— visualize the word <u>dance</u>
2.	**(3)**	absolute<u>ly</u>	— when you add the suffix <u>ly</u>, you keep the final e (exception: true—truly)
3.	**(2)**	rec<u>ei</u>ver	— the typical example of the <u>e-i</u> rule
4.	**(4)**	l<u>ei</u>sure	— one of the exceptions to the <u>e-i</u> rule
5.	**(2)**	la<u>bo</u>ratory	— think of the word <u>labor</u>
6.	**(5)**		— the word <u>lightening</u> means to get lighter, like a load
7.	**(3)**	scar<u>ce</u>ly	— the word is scar<u>ce</u>
8.	**(2)**	o<u>m</u>it	
9.	**(1)**	signifi<u>c</u>ant	— visualize the word <u>cant</u>
10.	**(5)**		
11.	**(1)**	appear<u>a</u>nce	— think of the word <u>ran</u>
12.	**(2)**	p<u>ie</u>ce	— the old favorite: a <u>pie</u>ce of <u>pie</u>!
13.	**(3)**	curi<u>o</u>sity	— the root word is curious, but it changes here
14.	**(3)**	de<u>ce</u>ive	— the <u>e-i</u> rule
15.	**(5)**		
16.	**(3)**	me<u>re</u>ly	
17.	**(3)**	happ<u>i</u>ness	— change the <u>y</u> to <u>i</u> before adding a suffix
18.	**(3)**	ar<u>gu</u>ment	— think of <u>gum</u>
19.	**(2)**	fat<u>al</u>	
20.	**(1)**	simil<u>ar</u>	
21.	**(3)**	<u>al</u>though	
22.	**(4)**	sym<u>pathy</u>	— visualize <u>path</u>

165

WRITING

23.	(1)	ben<u>e</u>fit	— think of the Latin root <u>bene</u>, meaning good or well
24.	(2)	begi<u>nn</u>ing	— visualize <u>inning</u>
25.	(3)	<u>dis</u>ease	— the prefix <u>dis</u> means not or away
26.	(3)	f<u>o</u>rty	
27.	(1)	pre<u>cede</u>	—think of the root <u>cede</u>, meaning to go
28.	(3)	o<u>f</u>ten	
29.	(5)		
30.	(1)	conv<u>e</u>nient	— this is a matter of an "eye-fix" <u>venient</u>
31.	(2)	refe<u>rr</u>ed	— accent on the second syllable
32.	(1)	soph<u>o</u>more	— a three-syllable word
33.	(1)	env<u>iro</u>nment	— visualize <u>iron</u>
34.	(3)	<u>medic</u>al	— think of <u>medic</u>
35.	(4)	rh<u>y</u>thm	
36.	(3)	off<u>er</u>ing	— add the suffix <u>ing</u> to the original word
37.	(3)	excit<u>ing</u>	— drop the final <u>e</u> when adding a suffix beginning with a vowel
38.	(4)	impos<u>si</u>ble	
39.	(4)	wri<u>t</u>ing	— one <u>t</u> keeps the long sound of the first vowel
40.	(1)	noti<u>ce</u>able	— the <u>e</u> keeps the soft sound of the <u>c</u>
41.	(2)	bound<u>a</u>ries	— a three-syllable word
42.	(2)	absen<u>ce</u>	
43.	(3)	tr<u>ie</u>s	— change the <u>y</u> to <u>i</u> before adding <u>es</u>
44.	(4)	ni<u>ce</u>ly	— keep the final <u>e</u> when adding the suffix <u>ly</u>
45.	(4)	cert<u>ai</u>n	
46.	(3)	sep<u>a</u>rate	— think of <u>apart</u>
47.	(4)	occu<u>r</u>s	
48.	(2)	pro<u>f</u>essor	
49.	(3)	n<u>ie</u>ce	— the e-i rule
50.	(1)	r<u>i</u>diculous	— think of <u>rid</u>
51.	(3)	sudde<u>nn</u>ess	— retain the original word when adding the suffix
52.	(4)	equip<u>ment</u>	— add the suffix <u>ment</u> to the original word
53.	(3)	po<u>ss</u>ess	— remember the four <u>s</u>'s
54.	(4)	requir<u>e</u>ment	— add the suffix <u>ment</u> to the original word
55.	(1)	saf<u>e</u>ty	— add the suffix ty to the original word
56.	(4)	mana<u>g</u>ement	— add the suffix <u>ment</u> to the original word

ANSWERS AND ANALYSIS

57. **(5)**
58. **(4)** am**at**eur — **(3)** is the correct plural of <u>alley</u>
59. **(2)** coura**g**eous — the <u>e</u> keeps the soft sound of the <u>g</u>
60. **(2)** defin**i**tely — think of the word <u>finite</u>

EXERCISE ONE Sample: **(2)** deceit

1. **(1)** receive
2. **(3)** chief
3. **(3)** freight
4. **(2)** niece
5. **(4)** siege
6. **(1)** fierce
7. **(3)** fiend
8. **(4)** retrieve
9. **(5)**
10. **(3)** mischief

EXERCISE TWO

1. fanciest
2. Sundays
3. worrier
4. boundaries
5. happiness
6. days
7. quarries
8. Wednesdays
9. days
10. tried

EXERCISE THREE

1. encouraging
2. hopeful
3. happiest
4. disparaging
5. intensely
6. hoping; hopping
7. desirable
8. noticing; cringing

9. replacing
10. discouraging

EXERCISE FOUR

1. housewives'
2. fieldmice's
3. bats'
4. persons' (The word *people* is sometimes regarded as the plural of person; therefore, people's.)
5. wolves'
6. titles'
7. women's
8. ladies'
9. ours (Note: One of the possessive pronouns, ending in s, with no apostrophe.)
10. children's

EXERCISE FIVE

1. suffered—suffering
2. referred—referring
3. interfered—interfering
4. interred—interring
5. preferred—preferring
6. monitored—monitoring
7. audited—auditing
8. differed—differing
9. deferred—deferring
10. offered—offering

EXERCISE SIX

The *heroes' zeroes* were all shot down during *tornadoes*. On the ground they went down like *dominoes*. All their *theories* of flight were upset by their *leader's* (could also be *leaders'*) remarks. They treated the *principles* of formation flying like old *wives'* tales. But they all became *aces*.

ANSWERS AND ANALYSIS

PRETEST

1. The Panama Canal is in Panama.
2. Pat's Pizza Palace is in the shopping center.
3. I flew on an American Airlines jet when I went to California.
4. I saw the playoffs at Shea Stadium.
5. We received a free sample of Loveli, a new soap.
6. We often quote the Bible, but we don't read it often.
7. I wonder why they named that bridge the Verrazano.
8. Someday I would like to visit Australia and New Guinea.
9. Did you know that Lagos is the capital of Nigeria?
10. We toured through the old section of the city of Santo Domingo.
11. The government plans to rebuild the South Bronx.
12. The Mississippi is America's busiet waterway.
13. During World War II, the German Air Force destroyed Coventry.
14. Thanksgiving Day is a holiday in the United States.
15. I was amazed at the depth of Lake Tahoe.

EXERCISE ONE

1. **(2)** Irish refers to a nationality.
2. **(3)** Bob is the first name.
3. **(3)** The first word of a line of poetry should be capitalized.
4. **(3)** Beirut is the name of the city. (The word *mayor* is not capitalized because it is not used as part of the title.)
5. **(3)** The entire name of the product is Coca-Cola.

EXERCISE TWO

1. <u>T</u>he race for mayor in <u>N</u>ew <u>Y</u>ork <u>C</u>ity was an interesting one.
2. For the first time in a long while, an incumbent mayor was defeated. (Correct)
3. <u>E</u>d <u>K</u>och, a congressman from <u>M</u>anhattan, decided to run for <u>C</u>ity <u>H</u>all.
4. It was felt that with the support of the <u>B</u>lacks and the <u>J</u>ewish part of the population, he would win.
5. Actually, <u>K</u>och got support from the midtown areas between the <u>H</u>udson and <u>E</u>ast <u>R</u>ivers.

EXERCISE THREE

1. They drove south on the newly completed <u>F</u>lorida <u>S</u>tate <u>P</u>arkway.
2. <u>T</u>he party was being given by <u>D</u>r. and <u>M</u>rs. Grimaldi.
3. It was an honor to be greeted by <u>T</u>heir <u>R</u>oyal <u>M</u>ajesties.
4. Broadway is known throughout the world as the <u>G</u>reat <u>W</u>hite <u>W</u>ay.
5. Many immigrants grew up on <u>N</u>ew <u>Y</u>ork's <u>L</u>ower <u>E</u>ast <u>S</u>ide.

EXERCISE FOUR

1. **(1)** The first word in a sentence is capitalized.
2. **(4)** This is the name of a particular building.
3. **(4)** <u>Travels Through Patagonia</u> is the complete title.
4. **(4)** This is part of the name of the geographical location.
5. **(1)** The first word in a sentence is capitalized.

EXERCISE FIVE

1. "I told you," he said, "I'm taking a course in geography at <u>MIT</u>."
2. <u>W</u>hile taking Dental <u>H</u>ygiene at <u>R</u>utgers, he met <u>J</u>ane.
3. The survivors said their trust in the <u>A</u>lmighty saved them.
4. She became a specialist in higher mathematics.
5. Despite difficulties in grammar, he did his best work in <u>E</u>nglish.

EXERCISE SIX

1. **(3)** Municipal Building is the full name of the building.
2. **(3)** Camp David is the full name.
3. **(4)** The Poconos are a particular mountain range.
4. **(4)** The word <u>Win</u> is an important part of the title.
5. **(3)** Mark is part of the full name of the publisher—Hall, Mark and Fame.
6. **(3)** The name of the shopping area is Golden Acre.
7. **(4)** German refers to a nationality.
8. **(1)** Dr. is the abbreviation for a title.
9. **(4)** Hamburg is the name of a German city.
10. **(2)** This means a resident of Hamburg—like New Yorker.

ANSWERS AND ANALYSIS

PRETEST

1. What a stunning flower arrangment!
2. When did you hear about your exam?
3. Gee! I hated to hear that news.
4. You have to be kidding!
5. Move your chair closer to the table.
6. That old house is supposed to be haunted.
7. Just what did you mean by that remark?
8. Great! We've won the final game of the series.
9. His mother said the child was lazy, *or* His mother said, "The child was lazy."
10. Please come immediately!
11. The address is 331 Pierson St., Brooklyn, N.Y.
12. It is nice to see you again, Jack.
13. Yes, of course, you may come to our house on Tuesday.
14. That car has recently been painted, hasn't it?
15. You have to take the Ohio Turnpike or you will miss it.

EXERCISE ONE

1. He asked them if they had any cigarettes.
2. What was their answer?
3. They did answer, but he could not understand them.
4. He asked again what they had said.
5. They became angry, and they shouted at him.
6. Why did they answer so roughly?
7. They did not understand him, and he could not understand them.
8. How horrible!
9. Misunderstanding breeds fear, and fear creates hatred.
10. Absolutely!

EXERCISE TWO

1. (3) The cheerleaders seem spiritless, <u>and</u> I can see the reason why.
        The cheerleaders seem spiritless; I can see the reason why.

2. (2) Their coach has been changed several times, <u>and</u> the team has lost its aggressiveness.
        Their coach has been changed several times; the team has lost its aggressiveness.

3. **(2)** He said they played poor ball, <u>but</u> that is not the real reason.
   He said they played poor ball; that is not the real reason.

4. **(3)** I think he has received offers from other clubs, <u>but</u> he denies this.
   I think he has received offers from other clubs; he denies this.

5. **(3)** Only time will tell who is right, <u>but</u> I think I am.
   Only time will tell who is right; I think I am.

EXERCISE THREE

1. He was, I think, more upset about losing than he should have been.
2. Of course, that's easy for me to say. I have nothing to lose.
3. What if you had been in the same position? How would you have felt?
4. Dreadful!
5. Well, Woody, I feel that you came out pretty well.
6. Humph!
7. Of course, the cameramen were pretty upset. They always are.
8. It's true, however, that most witnesses agree with me.
9. Witnesses! What do they know?
10. When one fully considers all the facts, November 14, 1942, will be one of history's great dates.

EXERCISE FOUR

1. He said that I had said, "Frieda, my love, you are a bore."
2. What I did say was that I loved Frieda more.
3. You ask why I said what I said.
4. I say to you now, "What else could I have said?"
5. Love can lead to say strange things; love can make us do stranger things.
6. As the Good Book says, "Love thy neighbor as theyself."
7. But what, my friend, if one does not love one's self very much?
8. Then one goes to Shakespeare: "Physician, heal thyself."
9. Frieda said, "Did he not also say, 'Throw physic to the dogs'?"
10. Then, my friend, we will have healthy dogs. Isn't that true?

ANSWERS AND ANALYSIS

CHAPTER FOUR

PRETEST

1.	(2)	excitingly	— adverb modifying <u>told</u>
2.	(4)	are	— you <u>are</u> wrong
3.	(2)	running	— parallelism with <u>sending</u> is required
4.	(3)	me	— would not let <u>me</u>
5.	(3)	yours	— possessive without apostrophe — <u>yours</u>
6.	(2)	has	— subject-verb agreement: <u>one has</u>
7.	(5)		
8.	(2)	we	— <u>we</u> had to clean up
9.	(4)	hers	— possessive without apostrophe
10.	(3)	it's	— contraction for <u>it is</u>
11.	(1)	Regardless	— no such word as <u>irregardless</u>
12.	(4)	omit at	— there is no such expression as "Where is it <u>at</u>?"
13.	(5)		— <u>me</u> is the object of consisted <u>of</u>
14.	(3)	principles	— means rules
15.	(1)	to	— the expression is <u>try to</u> find; never use <u>try and</u>
16.	(1)	Since or because	— there is no such expression as <u>being that</u>
17.	(5)		
18.	(3)	is	— the subject is <u>pile</u>
19.	(3)	angry	— predicate adjective
20.	(4)	rising	
21.	(4)	others	— no possessive needed
22.	(3)	accepted	
23.	(3)	there	
24.	(5)		
25.	(3)	the will	— parallelism
26.	(3)	already	
27.	(1)	omit both	— more than two elements are involved
28.	(1)	you're	— contraction for <u>you are</u>
29.	(5)		
30.	(1)	its	— possessive without apostrophe

EXERCISE ONE

1. social scientists—psychologists—philosophers—TV—taste—country
2. defenders—TV—medium—choice—people
3. fault—producers—public—violence—sex—entertainment
4. movies—programs—millions—viewers
5. change—taste—morals—programs—land

EXERCISE TWO

deal—groaning—Metropolitan Opera House—Saturday afternoon—Osie Hawkins—Sherrill Milnes—*Eugene Onegin*—groaning—baritone—Mr. Milnes—performance

EXERCISE THREE

1. Paul told *his* father, Steve, that *he* ought to play golf.
2. Steve explained that *he* could not play golf.
3. Steve's wife told *her* husband that *he* and *his* son should both play golf on Sundays, so that *she* could have some peace.

EXERCISE FOUR

1. They offered Donald and *me* a ride to town. (They offered *me*.)
2. Donald and *I* refused. (*I* refused.)
3. Then *he* and Timmy drove off. (*He* drove off.)
4. We noticed that Timmy and *he* were angry.

EXERCISE FIVE

1. He spoke to *whoever* was willing to listen. (*He/she* was willing. Be careful of examples like this.)
2. *Whom* did you say taught you how to throw a pass? (You said you taught *him/her*.)
3. Where did you go, and to *whom* did you speak? (You spoke to *him/her*.)
4. *Who* shall I say called you? (Shall I say *he/she* called you?)
5. I don't care *whom* you tell about it.
6. The men and women *who* have been elected are quite honest.
7. *Whoever* laughs last usually laughs best.
8. For *whom* did you vote?
9. Do you know anyone *who* can keep a secret?
10. I have no idea as to *who* will be chosen.

ANSWERS AND ANALYSIS

EXERCISE SIX

1. she—her
2. their—her
3. They—their—their—her—their
4. This—his
5. It—he—I—her—myself

EXERCISE SEVEN

1. her
2. She
3. its
4. its
5. its
6. their
7. their
8. her
9. their
10. his—he

EXERCISE EIGHT

1. she
2. they
3. their
4. she
5. them
6. They
7. her
8. they
9. her
10. they
11. her

EXERCISE NINE

1. *comes*—action; *to observe*—action; *are*—state of being
2. *is*—state of being
3. *could fly*—action
4. *are*—state of being
5. *seemed*—state of being; *is*—state of being

EXERCISE TEN

1. grew, grown
2. rise, risen
3. lie, lay
4. lie, lied
5. threw, thrown
6. burst, burst
7. wake, woke or waked
8. lend, lent
9. flew, flown
10. bear, borne

EXERCISE ELEVEN

1. had burst
2. will attend
3. are leaving
4. has risen
5. destroyed

EXERCISE TWELVE

1. has repaired
2. towers
3. am washing
4. has seen
5. had eaten

EXERCISE THIRTEEN

1. is
2. is
3. is
4. match
5. is

EXERCISE FOURTEEN

1. had mixed
2. has begun
3. will leave
4. wrung

ANSWERS AND ANALYSIS

5. had shaken
6. will instruct
7. has gone
8. acted
9. had irritated
10. had swollen

EXERCISE FIFTEEN

1. gleaming, slim, much
2. large, vast
3. great, huge
4. spindly
5. surprising, little
6. many, deliberate
7. NONE
8. beautiful, many
9. harshest, silent (pred. adj.)
10. several

EXERCISE SIXTEEN

1. most gracefully
2. stronger
3. highest
4. small—cleverer (more clever *is also accepted*)
5. keenest
6. largest
7. faster
8. foolishly

EXERCISE SEVENTEEN

1. He was unwilling to *accept* my gift.
2. I had bought it in a Moroccan *bazaar*.
3. It was really my *advice* that changed his mind
4. And that in itself was a rather *bizarre* **matter.**
5. It is usually very difficult to *advise* him about anything.
6. But since he was annoyed, all I said only served to *aggravate* him.
7. Actually, I had made absolutely no *allusion* to his attitude.
8. Even that admission did little to *alter* his opinion.
9. I had spoken to him any *number* of times.
10. If he continues this way, he will *burst* with frustration.

11. I *have been* there often.
12. This sensitivity was something he had had *to bear*.
13. *Because* he was my friend, I tried to understand.
14. From inside, he ordered them to *bring* the boxes from the yard to him.
15. But he did say he would speak to no one *except* me.

EXERCISE EIGHTEEN

1. They were *dying* to meet the star.
2. But he had already *deserted* the stage.
3. He regarded giving autographs as a *capital* offense.
4. Of *course*, he enjoyed performing.
5. It was hoped he would receive his just *deserts*.
6. But he usually refused to take anyone's *counsel*.
7. He was *continually* getting into trouble.
8. Trouble never seemed to bother his *conscience*.
9. He always had a rather *coarse* attitude.

EXERCISE NINETEEN

1. We were pleased by the visit of the *eminent* doctor.
2. The vessels were lost in a *naval* encounter.
3. This has *obligated* my young brother to finish his homework.
4. The actor had *led* a glamorous life.
5. She **pleaded** with her parents to *let* her make her own mistakes.
6. She felt a sense of fear *envelop* them.
7. But I noticed that as the visit grew *imminent*, the boy appeared to *lose* his enthusiasm.
9. At first I thought this was a *feint* to divert attention.
9. But by the time the doctor arrived, the truth *lay* in another direction.
10. During the visit, the kid was wrapped in an *envelope* of shyness.

EXERCISE TWENTY

1. Henry VIII was one of England's greatest rulers of the *past*.
2. He was rarely at *peace* with his wives.
3. His *principal* worry was that they were not faithful.
4. One could almost *prophesy* that he would behead them.
5. The *personnel* of his court were constantly uneasy.
6. On *principle*, during his *reign*, there were marriages and beheadings.

ANSWERS AND ANALYSIS

7. This, naturally, disturbed the *quiet* of England.
8. The ladies of the court had much to *learn* from their king.
9. It was uncomfortable to *sit* on the queen's throne.
10. The throne was frequently the start of the *route* to the scaffold.

CHAPTER FIVE

PRETEST

1. (3) It is the job which provided her with an income. The use of the word *thus* in the original sentence makes the sentence unclear.
2. (2) After the initial verb *hopes,* the infinitive form is used.
3. (5) No change is required since the entire sequence is in the past tense.
4. (3) This is the only choice which is a complete sentence.
5. (1) This removes the dangling participle.
6. (4) The expression is "Have you ever visited . . . ?"
7. (1) The participial phrase *becoming angry* is the subject. The use of the pronoun *that* is incorrect and confusing.
8. (1) Two actions are in the past, one preceding the other.
9. (2) The correlative *neither* is followed by *nor.*
10. (5) This is correct because the construction is parallel.
11. (3) Two past tenses are called for — one the past perfect, the other the simple past.
12. (4) The subject is the singular noun *pile,* which requires a singular verb.
13. (2) The clause should modify *I.*
14. (5) The introductory clause modifies *they.*
15. (3) This is the correct sequence of tenses.
16. (4) To answer this question, you must know the correct spelling of the word *their.* In addition, the adverb *obviously* must be placed next to the verb *had lost.*
17. (5) The sequence is simple past tense and past perfect tense to indicate two actions in the past, one preceding the other.
18. (4) In the other choices, the modifier is misplaced. Obviously, the building was not in their car.
19. (3) The dangling participle is corrected by this answer.
20. (3) The present perfect tense is used.
21. (1) The sequence is past tense and past perfect tense.
22. (4) Two elements are involve here keeping the tenses consistent in the past and eliminating the dangling participle.
23. (2) This is the only complete sentence.
24. (4) This corrects the dangling participle.
25. (1) This is the only complete sentence.

ANSWERS TO EXERCISES

EXERCISE ONE

1. sentence fragment
2. sentence fragment
3. sentence
4. sentence
5. sentence fragment

EXERCISE TWO

1. simple subject: visit
   complete subject: my mother's visit to Poland
2. simple subject: victory
   complete subject: a hard-fought victory against great odds
3. compound subject: Lynnette, Jane
   complete subject: Lynnette and Jane
4. simple subject: dress
   complete subject: the dress in the department store window
5. simple subject: labels
   complete subject: labels in clothing

EXERCISE THREE

1. paints of sixteen different colors
2. Juan, Russell's nephew
3. who
4. my cousin
5. you (understood subject)

EXERCISE FOUR

1. repaired
2. whined, yelped
3. did call
4. was
5. have spoken

EXERCISE FIVE

1. DO—gifts; IO—them
2. DO—them

3. DO—dress
4. DO—radio; IO—them
5. DO—him

EXERCISE SIX

1. sentence fragment
2. sentence
3. sentence
4. sentence fragment
5. sentence fragment
6. sentence
7. sentence fragment
8. sentence
9. sentence fragment
10. sentence

EXERCISE SEVEN

1. trip—S; aunt's—O; him—O
2. experience—S
3. effort—S
4. athlete—S; injuries—O
5. Success—S; happiness—O; sadness—O
6. cookies—O
7. feast—O; brother—O
8. Everyone—S; Hustle—O; skill—O
9. search—S
10. people—S; problems—O

EXERCISE EIGHT

1. in; to
2. with
3. for
4. with; in
5. to; of
6. after
7. to; to; for
8. by; for
9. on; in; of
10. between; of

182   WRITING

EXERCISE NINE

1. shopping, walking, and *visiting* . . .
2. careful choice, wise pricing, and *good management,*
3. Newer ideas . . . , more skilled mechanics . . . , better relations . . . , and *the desire to increase sales* . . .
4. why he is living, why he is cared for, why his parents . . . , **and** *why he must do* . . .
5. the glory of Greece, the grandeur of Rome, and *the traditions* of England

EXERCISE TEN

1. S
2. S
3. Cx
4. S
5. Cp
6. S
7. S

EXERCISE ELEVEN

1. Correct
2. Giggling all the way, *they* almost crashed the plane.
3. Approaching the airport, *they* saw the lights.
4. Correct
5. *Having* cut off the engine, the crew . . .
6. Correct
7. Correct
8. Correct
9. Puzzled and angered by all this, *the owner* closed the store.
10. Correct

CHAPTER SIX

PRETEST

1. (3) This choice retains the proper tone of the sentence. The word *incarcerate (4)* is both too elaborate and inaccurate, since it means "to put into jail."
2. (2) This removes the double negative.
3. (3) The other choices are incorrect meanings. In addition, *averting* and *evading* are a little high-toned.

ANSWERS AND ANALYSIS

4. **(3)** The use of the pronoun *it* in the original sentence is confusing. *(1)* is wrong because the pronoun is indefinite.
5. **(4)** This word retains the tone of the sentence.
6. **(3)** This expression is on the same level as the other descriptions.
7. **(4)** *Twirling*, while expressing an action similar to *diddling*, is a more formal word.
8. **(1)** *Urged* expresses the emotion that is described.
9. **(2)** *Fact* is the subject of the verb *shows*.
10. **(3)** The use of the term *they* introduces a confusing and indefinite quality into the sentence.
11. **(3)** This is of the same tone as the rest of the sentence.
12. **(2)** The other answers introduce a colloquial element which is not suitable.
13. **(3)** The idiom is *to center . . . on*.
14. **(1)** This is the proper tone. *(3)* is wrong because it is not clear who was discourteous.
15. **(2)** The idiom is *different from*.
16. **(5)** This sentence is complete and clear as it stands.
17. **(3)** One *steals something from* someone or some place.
18. **(3)** It is again a matter of tone.

SAMPLE EXERCISE

Note: Because this is essentially a matter of taste, there is no absolute right or wrong. It becomes principally a matter of level and strength of expression.

Last Saturday, which was a *splendid* day, we took a *wonderful* trip. We went to visit that *incredible* center of buildings, *exciting* displays, *beautiful* fountains, and *entertaining* things to do — Disneyland. Even though the traffic was *extremely heavy*, with a couple of *crunching* traffic jams on the way, it was really a *very pleasant* ride.

Once we took a wrong turn and got caught in a *terrible* mess. The cars were coming at us from all sides. They were blowing their horns and making a *frightening* racket. Luckily for us a *policeman* came along, and he was *kind* enough to stop the traffic so we could turn around and get back into line for the parking lot.

That was only the start of what turned out to be a *memorable* day of traveling and eating all kinds of *delicious* things and seeing the *marvelous* displays in that *amazing* place — Disneyland.

Note: Some of the words from the original paragraphs are retained. It is frequently the overuse of a term that makes it lose its power; a balanced use of words is certainly permitted.

CHAPTER SEVEN
PRETEST

1. **(2)** This sentence is the topic sentence. Its function is to tell what the paragraph will discuss.
2. **(3)** This transition word emphasizes the point of view of the author.
3. **(2)** These two sentences, in their present position, establish the pattern of development of the argument presented.
4. **(1)** There is no need to introduce any personal pronouns since the entire discussion is conducted on an objective level.
5. **(3)** Sentence 2 provides a specific example of the reasons for the author's being "shocked" by her discoveries.
6. **(5)** It is clear that the plural sense is required.
7. **(1)** An adverb is called for to modify the adjective *different*.
8. **(4)** The correct order of the sentences in this paragraph is 4, 3, 2, 1.
9. **(1)** Sentence 2 provides an illustration of the meaning of the first, or topic, sentence.
10. **(5)**
11. **(1)** The word *however* would indicate a change in direction. The simple statement continues the thought of the preceding sentences.
12. **(1)** This further demonstrates the author's point.
13. **(1)** Sentences 5 and 7 indicate further development of the discussion, but each introduces a different element in the point of view expressed.
14. **(3)** The colon shows that there will be a listing of reasons and illustrations.
15. **(5)** The word means to be accepted by the general public.
16. **(2)** Special words or foreign terms are set off by quotation marks.
17. **(2)** See Answer 13 above.
18. **(1)** This word links what precedes and what follows it.
19. **(1)**

EXERCISE ONE

1. **(5)**
2. **(2)** The correct expression is *because of* since this is a cause and effect relationship.
3. **(3)** The word *however* signals a contrast or change in direction. What is needed here is a word like *also*.

EXERCISE TWO

1. John's brother was considerably older than he, *but* John was a much better dancer. *As a result,* there was a considerable amount of envy between them. *Despite this,* they were still very fond of each other.
2. *Because* the need for control of bad air was established years ago, means for

handling the problem were discussed seriously. *However*, additional sources of bad air were developed. *As a result*, the government itself stepped into the matter.
3. The problem of peace in the Mideast concerns the world. There are some, *however*, who constantly seem to be playing with fire. *Therefore*, many of the steps toward peace are made difficult. It is hoped that cool heads and minds remain on top.
4. *Because* an understanding of words stems from constant reading, it is important to concentrate on teaching reading at all levels. *Consequently*, introducing simplified reading texts at an early age will help. *However*, it is not a problem for the schools alone.
5. Growing older makes one sensitive to weather changes. *For example*, what was once regarded as "brisk" weather becomes "freezing." *As a result*, many people seek to move to warmer sections of the country. *Therefore*, the sun belt has become a booming area of population growth.

CHAPTER EIGHT
EXERCISE ONE

1. a noun meaning a lack of ability:
    prefix *in*—not
    suffix *ence*—noun clue meaning the quality of

2. an adverb meaning without stopping:
    prefix *in*—not
    stem *cess*—going, moving
    suffix *ly*—adverb clue

3. an adjective meaning going backward:
    prefix *re*—back
    stem *gress*—to go
    suffix *ive*—adjective clue

4. a noun meaning heat treatment:
    prefix *dia*—through, penetrating
    stem *therm*—heat
    suffix *y*—noun clue

5. an adjective meaning underground:
    prefix *sub*—under
    stem *terre*—earth, ground
    suffix *an*—adjective clue

6. an adjective meaning created, artificial:
   prefix *syn*—brought together, created
   stem *thet*—to make, place
   suffix *ic*—adjective clue

7. a noun meaning sound writing:
   prefix *phono*—sound
   stem *gram*—writing

8. a verb meaning to turn back:
   prefix *re*—back
   stem *vert*—to turn

9. an adjective meaning not believing:
   prefix *in*—not
   stem *cred*—to believe
   suffix *ous*—adjective clue

10. a noun meaning a missile, something hurled:
    prefix *pro*—out, forth
    stem *ject*—to throw
    suffix *ile*—noun clue

EXERCISE TWO

1. prefix *anti*—against
   stem *path*—feeling
   suffix *etic*—adjective clue

2. prefix *poly*—many
   suffix *gon*—noun clue

3. prefix *con*—toward, to
   stem *ver*—to turn
   suffix *sion*—noun clue

4. prefix *in*—not
   stem *fidel*—faithful, trust
   suffix *ity*—noun clue

ANSWERS AND ANALYSIS

5. prefix *bene*—good, well
   stem *dict*—to say, speak
   suffix *ion*—noun clue

6. prefix *inter*—between
   stem *mit*—to send, place
   suffix *ent*—adjective clue

7. prefix *extra*—outside, in addition to
   stem *sens*—feeling
   suffix *ory*—adjective clue

8. prefix *un*—not
   stem *sym*—to, toward, with
   stem *path*—feeling
   suffix *etic*—adjective clue

9. prefix *in*—in, into, toward
   stem *voca*—to call
   suffix *tion*—noun clue

10. prefix *bi*—two
    stem *partis*—sharing with, leaning toward
    suffix *an*—noun clue

11. stem *auto*—self
    suffix *nomous*—adjective clue

12. prefix *a*—not, without, lacking
    stem *moral*—ethics, judging good and evil
    suffix *ity*—noun clue

13. stem *transit*—passing through, moving
    suffix *ion*—noun clue meaning the quality of
    suffix *al*—adjective clue (Note: The final suffix shapes the word.)

14. prefix *in*—not
    stem *tract*—to draw, to pull, to lead
    suffix *able*—adjective clue

15. prefix *inter*—between
    stem *ject*—to hurl, throw
    suffix *ion*—noun clue

POSTTEST

SPELLING, PUNCTUATION, AND CAPITALIZATION

1. **(1)** fiend
2. **(2)** agreeable
3. **(2)** supervise Note: The word *advise* is the verb; the noun is *advice*.
4. **(1)** mission*a*ry
5. **(2)** evidently This is a four-syllable word.
6. **(2)** procedure
7. **(1)** inconvenient This misspelling is common because of an "eye" error.
8. **(4)** hygiene Three words are pronounced sit: cite, sight, site
9. **(4)** tonnage The doubled *n* keeps the short sound of the vowel.
10. **(2)** unveiling
11. **(1)** *H*is The first word of the sentence must be capitalized.
12. **(4)** This should be a semicolon since it continues the pattern of the compound sentence.
13. **(4)** The sentence is a question.
14. **(1)** No capital is necessary since this is a common noun.
15. **(5)**
16. **(3)** Such an abbreviation must be capitalized, since it is part of a title.
17. **(5)** Brother Francis is capitalized because it is a name.
18. **(5)**
19. **(3)** A comma should be used with the word *and*.
20. **(5)** The word Capitol is capitalized since it is the name of a particular building.

GRAMMAR AND USAGE

1. **(4)** In formal English, a sentence may not end with a preposition.
2. **(4)** The objective form must be used after the preposition *of*. Therefore, *me*.
3. **(3)** yours
4. **(3)** each This must agree in number with the pronoun *she*, which follows.
5. **(5)**
6. **(4)** I *My brother and I* had to make up the homework. The *subject form* is called for.
7. **(2)** really An *adverb* modifies another adverb.
8. **(4)** had raised Two actions are in the past, one preceding the other. (*Had raised* precedes *was*.) The *past perfect* is used.
9. **(1)** had learned The *past perfect* is used here.
10. **(3)** his learning A possessive pronoun is used before a gerund.
11. **(4)** unhappy A predicate adjective follows a linking verb.
12. **(4)** The expression should be *to whom*.

ANSWERS AND ANALYSIS

13. **(5)**
14. **(4)** principles
15. **(5)**
16. **(5)** The verb agrees with the part of the subject to which it is closer.
17. **(4)** his *Everbody* is singular.
18. **(4)** gets Shipment is a singular subject.
19. **(1)** while she was driving This is a case of a dangling participle.
20. **(2)** the latter's As it stands the antecedent of the second *her* is unclear.
21. **(3)** who *Who* is the subject of the verb *was. He thought* is a parenthetical expression.
22. **(4)** her The objective form appears after the verb *permit.*
23. **(1)** as good as
24. **(1)** you're *You're* is the contraction for *you are.*

DICTION AND STYLE

1. **(#)** Since we are speaking about a "gang," the level of speech is probably lower than that indicated by the other choices. This is slang.
2. **(2)** The other choices are too formal.
3. **(3)** While this phrase—*dreadfully unkind*—sounds somewhat formal, it fits in with the use of the word *perpetrate.*
4. **(1)** *Like* or *as* is the first word of a *simile.*
5. **(3)** There is no such expression as *being that.*
6. **(3)** The correct spelling is *all right.*
7. **(1)**
8. **(3)** Avoid the double negative.
9. **(4)** Remember that there is no such word as *ir*regardless.
10. **(5)** The meaning here is that *all (of them) were ready.*
11. **(3)** The action of a human being is attributed to an object.
12. **(3)** It is unlikely that the first two predicate adjectives would be followed by such a formal word as perspicacious.

SENTENCE STRUCTURE

1. **(4)** The original sentence contains a dangling participle. It sounds as though the song was doing the listening.
2. **(2)** The original sentence makes it sound as though the condition had lost all her money.
3. **(3)** Combining the two related sentences into one makes for a better expression.
4. **(4)** The gerund phrase *being challenged* is the subject.
5. **(2)** The misplaced modifier is corrected by this form. Obviously the station was not pulled by an engine.

6. **(1)** This correction avoids the awkward repetition of the original.
7. **(2)** *Accept* means to receive; *except* means to omit.
8. **(5)** This is the verb form meaning to *suggest*. The *noun* is *advice*.
9. **(3)** The construction must be parallel: *overbearing, demanding,* and *humiliating.*
10. **(4)** This is the only choice having parallel structure. In addition, *And war too* is not a sentence.
11. **(2)** The possessive pronoun is used with the gerund.

LOGIC AND ORGANIZATION

1. **(1)** This sentence establishes the theme of the paragraph.
2. **(5)** The word *too* indicates a continuation of the thought of the first sentence, with an illustration.
3. **(3)** The semicolon establishes the compound form. Not using any transition word makes this more concise.
4. **(3)** This expression typically introduces an illustration of what is being discussed.
5. **(4)** Each of these sentences introduces a new aspect of the original thought.
6. **(4)** Sentence 8 establishes this fact very plainly.
7. **(4)** This is completely irrelevant.
8. **(4)** The use of the word *alone* indicates that some other threat has been discussed previously.
9. **(4)** A change of direction and interest is indicated by the word *However.*
10. **(1)** This example does not belong in this paragraph since *Torrey Canyon* was involved in one of the great pollution disasters.
11. **(1)** This sentence is an illustration of the statement made in the preceding sentence.
12. **(1)** It is clear that this conclusion culminates the thought of the paragraph.